PRESERVING DIESEL HYDRAULIC LOCOMOTIVES
1977–82

STEVE CROWTHER

First published 2025

Amberley Publishing
The Hill, Stroud,
Gloucestershire, GL5 4EP

www.amberley-books.com

Copyright © Steve Crowther, 2025

The right of Steve Crowther to be identified as the Author of this work has been asserted in accordance with the Copyright, Designs and Patents Act 1988.

All rights reserved. No part of this book may be reprinted or reproduced or utilised in any form or by any electronic, mechanical or other means, now known or hereafter invented, including photocopying and recording, or in any information storage or retrieval system, without the permission in writing from the Publishers.

ISBN: 978 1 3981 2573 5 (print)
ISBN: 978 1 3981 2574 2 (ebook)

British Library Cataloguing in Publication Data.
A catalogue record for this book is available from the British Library.

Typeset in 10pt on 13pt Celeste.
Typesetting by Hurix Digital Ltd., India.
Printed in the UK.

Appointed GPSR EU Representative: Easy Access System Europe Oü, 16879218
Address: Mustamäe tee 50, 10621, Tallinn, Estonia
Contact Details: gpsr.requests@easproject.com, +358 40 500 3575

Contents

	Introduction	4
1	Background	5
2	Time Is Running Out	7
3	The Light Begins to Shine Again	9
4	Swindon Works Revisited	11
5	Time to Move	19
6	Trusting Times	25
7	Feeling the Cold	28
8	And Then There Were Three	34
9	Here, There and Everywhere	42
10	Onwards and Upwards	53
11	Testing Times	62
12	Pastures New	69
13	Money and Politics	75
14	Turning the Corner	82
15	A Change of Direction	88
16	Conclusion	93
	Acknowledgements	96

Introduction

After some consideration and various requests, I have decided to put pen to paper in order to give people some insight into the early years of diesel preservation. However, I must stress that this only revolves around my own relatively short experience with three diesel hydraulic locomotives: D1048 *Western Lady*, D1041 *Western Prince* and D832 *Onslaught*. All photographs were taken by the author.

These were not the first diesel hydraulics to be preserved. The pioneers in this field were Colin Massingham with Warship D821 *Greyhound*, the Western Locomotive Association with D1062 *Western Courier*, Richard Holdsworth with D1013 *Western Ranger*, the Diesel & Electric Group with Hymek D7017 then later D7018 and the Diesel Traction Group with D1015 *Western Champion* and D7029.

Full credit must be given to these people for having the foresight, courage, time and money to save these locomotives for future generations to enjoy.

I hope I have been able to correctly remember the following events as they unfolded, but if any errors have occurred, please accept my apologies. After all, it was over forty-five years ago.

Some readers may recall that the late Adrian Curtis, the renowned Western historian, published a much shorter version of this story in *Classic Diesels & Electrics* magazine some years ago.

Many books have been written about diesel hydraulic locomotives, detailing their design, construction, technical details, introduction and service lives, which I do not wish to duplicate here. This book mainly deals with three locomotives after their service lives had ended and their preservation was secured.

1
Background

I grew up in the north-west town of Newton-le-Willows, famous for its Vulcan locomotive works. The town at this time was like many others: a thriving, busy place. In addition to the Vulcan Foundry it had the Viaduct Wagon Works, a printing works, a sugar works, a biscuit machinery factory and Parkside Colliery. Workers were brought in from the surrounding areas, including Warrington, Wigan, Leigh, Atherton, etc. The town lies close to the West Coast Main Line and on the Liverpool–Manchester line. My own interest in railways began with trainspotting locally; Vulcan and Winwick areas were my favourite haunts. I could cycle there in around fifteen minutes and would meet other local lads with the same interests. In fact, this is where I first met my long-time friend Bernard Worrall (of which more later). Additionally, I enjoyed a bike ride alongside the canal from Winwick to the local shed at Warrington Dallam 8b to see which locos were about and spot the ones we had missed. It was a busy place at this time, with anything from tank engines to Pacifics coming and going. Also, brand-new Type 1 diesels (later Class 20s) could often be seen there fresh from the Vulcan Works.

Those times in the mid-1960s were fascinating as you could spend hours watching the numerous steam locos, from the mighty Duchesses and Britannias to Jubilees, Black 5s, 8Fs, 9Fs and early diesels such as the Class 40s, which at the time were known to us as Big Ds. I also remember seeing new Class 47s in a pink undercoat on test runs from Crewe Works. The early Peaks (later Class 44s) also made an appearance.

The Vulcan Works were a little bit special to me. I would often cycle down and see a brand-new English Electric Type 3 or Type 1 (Class 37 and Class 20 as they became known in later years) outside the works with their gleaming paintwork waiting to enter BR service. Class 73s were also a common sight at that time. I often saw a Class 20/73 combination running away from the works en route to their new life with BR. Both of my parents were employed at the works at different times. This occasionally allowed me access inside where I could see both diesel and electric locos under construction; I was also fortunate to see prototypes GT3 and DP2. Incidentally, after leaving school my mother got me an apprenticeship there, but eventually I decided the factory environment was not for me and I left and went into agricultural engineering where I've been to this day.

In the mid to late 1960s my friend Bernard and I went on numerous organised coach trips around the country to loco sheds and depots. Firstly, with the LCGB (Locomotive Club of Great Britain), then later with the Salford Loco Club. It was during these trips that we could savour the delights of the diesel hydraulic classes up close at such far-flung places as Landore (Swansea), Cardiff Canton, Bristol Bath Road, Plymouth Laira and Penzance. Prior to this I have vivid memories of a ride behind D1073 *Western Bulwark* to Taunton in July 1964 while en route to visit an aunt in Braunton, North Devon. During this visit I also saw Hymeks D7095, D7096 and D7100 and Class 22s D6308, D6316, D6339 and D6342 on the Ilfracombe line. These memories stayed with me and fostered my interest in diesel hydraulics.

I didn't realise at the time how fortunate I was to have seen these locomotives in action, as their reign was sadly short-lived due to BR wanting to rid itself of the diesel hydraulic classes. The first Class 22s and D600 Warships were taken out of service and scrapped in 1968 – the same year that steam ended. This was followed by the first two D800 Warship Class being scrapped in 1969 after which their demise gathered pace into the 1970s.

2
Time Is Running Out

Fast-forward to the late 1970s and only the Westerns were left in service, and even they were disappearing fast. The first one was taken out of service in 1973. Bernard and I were frequent visitors to the West Country to photograph and ride behind as many as we could, usually travelling down in Bernard's Ford Capri. We also holidayed together and would ride behind them along the sea wall at Dawlish and Teignmouth down to Paignton and Plymouth. On one occasion, having travelled down from the north, we arrived at Exeter in the very early morning and managed to get a cab ride around the depot in D1015 *Western*

In this view the author stands alongside D1053 *Western Patriarch* at Plymouth Laira depot on 29 August 1976.

Champion. Seeing all of the cab desk lights illuminated in the darkness was magical to us, but unfortunately I can't remember the name of the friendly driver. However, it is a lasting memory.

Amongst other many happy memories I have riding behind the Westerns is the time on 7 September 1976 when I travelled behind D1033 *Western Trooper* from Plymouth to Newquay. The sound and smell from the loco climbing up the Luxulyan Valley was simply unforgettable. This loco still remains a firm favourite of mine and many people referred to it as 'Super Trooper'.

In their final years, many railtours were organised using these locos as their popularity grew at an amazing rate. We went on as many of these as we could, including The Western Southwestern, Western Finale, Western Requiem, Western China Clay (a personal favourite of mine) and Western Talisman until the very last tour, Western Tribute, organised by British Rail, which ran on 26 February 1977. On our return to Paddington that night, having been uncoupled from their train, we watched as D1013 *Western Ranger* and D1023 *Western Fusilier* disappeared into the darkness, bringing the curtain down on the BR hydraulic era. This really was a poignant moment as I'm sure many who were there will testify. That was it, it was all over. It was the end and a big light had gone out, or perhaps not quite?

3

The Light Begins to Shine Again

In late 1977 Bernard and I visited the annual Wigan model railway exhibition. Remarkably, a gentleman called Dave Rigby had a stand there with information on his wish to purchase and preserve D1048 *Western Lady*. We chatted about it between ourselves, then approached him and asked if he would like any help in his quest. He happily agreed to our offer. After a discussion with him we drove home not really knowing how things would unfold or what we were letting ourselves in for. At this time Bernard was living in Newton-le-Willows and I was living in nearby Ashton-in-Makerfield.

In January 1978, Dave contacted me with a request for Bernard and myself to join him and a chap called Paul at a meeting in Bristol on the 29th. Here we met Pam Keck and others from the Western Loco Association in order to try and get some idea as to what may be involved in buying a Western.

Having received a tender form from BR for D1048 on 27 March, Dave, Paul, Bernard and I had a trip down to Newton Abbot in Devon to inspect the loco, which was located inside the old works with classmate D1041 *Western Prince*. D1010 *Western Campaigner* and D1013 *Western Ranger* had also been stored there, but had by now left for their new lives in preservation. The place seemed eerily quiet as we had a good look around *Lady*. Although we were technically inexperienced, by the time we left we were satisfied with what we had seen. Incidentally, *Lady* had been withdrawn as 'serviceable' whereas *Prince* had been withdrawn as 'unserviceable' with a burnt-out dynostart. Following our visit, Dave tendered for D1048 and was successful. I believe he paid around £6,000 for it, but I'm unable to confirm this. Plans were then made to move both locos up to Swindon Works. However, upon examination of D1041, damage to the A-end final drive was discovered which necessitated some repair work that would have to be carried out before the loco could move. This work was done by BR at a cost of £150 after which a date was set for the transfer of both locos to Swindon Works.

Above: D1048 *Western Lady* is seen inside the old works at Newton Abbot during our visit on 27 March 1978.

Below: Dave, Bernard and Paul pose with *Lady*.

4

Swindon Works Revisited

On Wednesday 28 June Dave, Bernard and I drove down to Bristol where we left the car and caught a train for the remainder of the journey to Newton Abbot to 'ride' D1048 up to Swindon. We were almost at our destination when Dave shouted, 'They've just passed us!' This was on the sea wall section near Teignmouth. On our arrival at Newton Abbot, we found out to our dismay that the convoy had left early. 'Oh bugger' and other such comments were said! After some discussion with the station staff, we found out the convoy would be recessed at Taunton, so a plan B was made. We were granted permission to ride up to Taunton in the rear cab of the loco due in with the next parcels train. This train pulled

Dave chats to the driver of 50048 *Dauntless* during a stop at Exeter St Davids whilst en route to Taunton on 28 June 1978.

in with 50048 *Dauntless* at the front (quite ironic having the same number 48, we thought). I remember when getting aboard the loco the driver said, 'Don't touch anything', as if we would. It was a cloudy day and apart from a stop at Exeter the journey was uneventful. On arrival at Taunton we found 31165, 31135, D1048 and D1041 stabled in the sidings. We walked across and met the owner of D1041, Dave Eddleston. We had a friendly chat, during which it emerged Dave hadn't really got a concrete plan for his loco, and to be honest neither had we for ours. However, Dave said he was going to take his loco to Didcot where the Hymek D7018 he previously owned was located, but in the end things worked out very differently, as we shall see.

We left Taunton in the late evening and travelled overnight to Swindon, being recessed in every loop en route it seemed. We arrived around 6 a.m. in the pouring rain and were shunted onto the depot. Bizarrely, during these moves we witnessed a London-bound HST with power car No. 43035 leading collide with a parcels train being shunted near the station. The power car was subsequently removed and the remainder of the train was marshalled alongside us. With our locos safely on the depot, we left and made our way back to Bristol to collect the car for the drive home. The locos were moved into the works yard the following day.

Over the next few months we travelled down to Swindon to carry out work on D1048, which mainly involved making it look a lot more respectable bodywork wise and carrying out some mechanical repairs. To give some idea of our commitment, after checking my

This view was taken at Swindon after our arrival at 5.45 a.m. 31165, 31135, D1048 and D1041 stand in the early morning rain on 29 June 1978.

Above: D1048 and D1041 are stabled at Swindon on the wet morning of 29 June 1978.

Below: Dave Eddleston looks out from the cab of his loco at Swindon on 29 June 1978. He had always wanted to own a Western!

notes it seems we drove down from the north-west to Swindon and back on the following dates in 1978: 3 August, 6 August, 12/13 August, 20 August, 27 August, 10 September, 17 September, 24 September and 1 October. Each journey involved at least six to seven hours of travelling time, plus fuel for the trip (these days it would take a lot longer and be a lot more expensive!). However, by the end of these visits *Lady* was looking very different, so it was well worth the effort, I must say. Looking at the newly painted loco was a stark contrast to its classmates lying derelict in the works yard awaiting scrapping.

There are a couple of points of interest here. Firstly, we did have some occasional help with us on some trips, including my first wife, Linda; a colleague from work, Mick Spruce; Martin Ollie; and John Boyes, who worked for Dave Rigby at the time. Poor Dave Eddleston was always on his own, but we did of course help him. Regarding this, I feel I must point out that prior to meeting us Dave had been offered help with his loco on numerous occasions but sadly none of these offers came to fruition. Secondly, on our arrival on 27 August we found to our surprise the replica number and nameplates we had fitted to *Lady* had been stolen! These were actually made of fibreglass, so it was a mystery to us why they were taken. On Sunday 10 September, we had both D1041 and D1048 running in the yard. Each loco was running on both engines, so it was a bit like the old days for a while and brought back happy memories. Dave did move *Lady* up and down the yard a short way, then on 17 September we had *Lady* running again and were allowed to move up and down the yard a bit further this time. I must say, at this time the works staff were very accommodating towards us.

Whilst on visits to Swindon Works we would sometimes go to see Bill Jeffries in his office and would always admire the *Western Cavalier* nameplate mounted on the wall.

On 3 August 1978, D1048 stands outside the main works building at Swindon. Many photographs of hydraulics have been taken at this location over the years.

Above: Dave, Bernard and Martin are busy on the repaint of D1048 at Swindon on 13 August 1978.

Below: We took the opportunity to run up the engines in between painting duties on 13 August 1978.

Above: What a contrast when the sun shines! D1048 looking rather smart against classmate D1041, still in its withdrawn condition. They are photographed outside the weigh house at Swindon on 20 August 1978.

Below: Dave is seen moving D1048 a short distance in the works yard on 10 September 1978.

Above: Having painted over where the name and number plates had been, D1048 stands in the morning sun. This photo from 17 September 1978 shows what the class would have looked like if they hadn't carried names. In my opinion their appearance would have been quite bland without them. Dave and John can be seen in the cab.

Below: Dave slowly drives D1048 up the yard away from the weigh house on 17 September 1978. Many years later this building was transformed into a restaurant. All the other works buildings in this view are but a memory, the whole area having been redeveloped. The once mighty Swindon Works is sadly no more.

Above: A close-up of Dave at the controls of his loco on 17 September 1978.

Below: D1048 shares space in the weigh house with D7029 on 24 September 1978, which was there for a repaint, I believe.

5

Time to Move

During the months at Swindon, in addition to working on the loco we were trying to find a railway willing to accept a Western. One of the railways approached was the North Yorkshire Moors Railway and after negotiations they offered, at a meeting on 18 February 1978, to enter into an operating agreement with Dave, allowing him to bring *Lady* to the line. This was accepted and plans were drawn up to move the loco up there. The move was set for 6 and 7 October 1978. Meanwhile, Dave Eddleston still hadn't decided on a future for D1041. We did ask him to join forces with us, but Dave had to have some major work done on his loco, including an engine and bogie change, plus a pre-heater change, which was costly, so the time was not right for a move from the works. In many respects, it was located in the right place. As a matter of interest, the engine and bogie he eventually had fitted came from D1071 *Western Renown*.

In the early morning of Friday 6 October, myself, Bernard and Dave were once again at Swindon Works, having driven down in Dave's Austin Princess, which incidentally had the registration number TEN 48T. It was around 7 a.m. and the sun would soon be shining as *Lady* was stabled, ready for the move north coupled to a brake van. It was later decided that this would not be required, however, so it was uncoupled from the loco. Bernard and I fitted a replacement set of number and nameplates, then 31123 coupled up and did the usual brake tests, etc., and we were ready to roll. The plan was for myself and Dave to ride the loco up to Derby and Bernard would drive the car there, then I would swap with Bernard for the rest of the first day's journey to Thornaby. All went well.

On our arrival at Thornaby we had a lot of interest from the staff. After an overnight stay in a B&B, the following morning we went back to the depot to find *Lady* on the fuelling road having a top-up. If I remember correctly, I think they said they would book the fuel down to a shunter! Whatever they did, we were very grateful. 31143 now coupled on for our final move via Battersby to Grosmont. The move went well and we arrived at our new home safe and sound.

After our arrival, we had a gauging run to Pickering and back. Again, all went well. The following weekend, 14 and 15 October, we travelled up to Grosmont and prepared and started *Lady* for its first trips on the NYMR. We always had the same procedure for starting this great loco. Initially, we would get the pre-heaters fired up, then while we waited for the water temperature to rise, we would go in the engine room and undo the decompressors on each engine in turn and bar them over on the flywheel. When the correct temperature was reached and the oil pressure was up, we would then press the local start button in the engine room and turn each engine over a few times. This would allow any moisture/water to escape from the cylinders; we did have some water issues in one cylinder of engine at the time (I think B end). We would then tighten up all the decompressors and one of us would open the fuel rack while the other would observe each engine in turn as Dave gave the 'OK' from the cab, pressed the start button and away it went. We never had any trouble when starting it this way; the engines would always burst into life effortlessly. On Saturday the 14th we had a round trip to Pickering – *Lady's* first run in preservation. This was a great achievement for us and much enjoyed by the passengers onboard. The next day our only job was to take a steam crane from Grosmont to Pickering. On our return to Grosmont we shut down the loco before heading home.

During our first weeks at Grosmont something significant happened: we were approached by a young man asking if he could join our group. His name was Malcolm Kirkwood from Malton. He worked for BR in York as an electrician on locos, including Deltics, 37s, 47s, etc. 'An electrician,' we exclaimed. 'Wow, welcome aboard!' He was just what we needed. Bernard and I were more mechanically minded, but we were novices really, not having worked on locos before – prior to this Bernard had mainly worked on cars prior and myself on agricultural tractors. We just got stuck in and learnt as we went

It's approximately 7.30 a.m. on Friday 6 October and Bernard can be seen attaching the number plate of the second set of plates we had made for D1048.

Above: The sun is shining on 6 October 1978 as 31123 is coupled to D1048 ready for the trip to the NYMR. After some discussion it was decided the brake van would not be required, so a tail lamp was placed on our loco instead.

Below: A pause for signals at Standish Junction enabled me to get a quick photo from the embankment on 6 October 1978.

Above: It's the morning of Saturday 7 October 1978 at Thornaby as 31143 is coupled on to D1048 ready for the next part of the journey to Grosmont. Dave can be seen chatting to the driver before we leave.

Below: D1048 and 31143 are seen at Battersby en route to Grosmont on 7 October 1978.

Above: D1048 arrives at Pickering on Saturday 14 October 1978 with its first service train on the NYMR.

Below: It's 15 October 1978 and *Lady* is prepared for a second day of duties. With one engine running and a rather smoky pre-heater at work on the other, there is more smoke coming from *Lady* than the steam loco!

We are coupled to the steam crane as it is made ready for us to take to Pickering on 15 October 1978. Bernard can be seen with his head out of the engine room window, the engine room being one of his favourite places.

along. Having Malc along with us would be – and was – a godsend. At this point we now totalled five, with Dave Eddleston having decided to join forces with us. Our objective was to take care of two Western Class locos, D1041 and D1048, which were in different parts of the country. It was no mean task, but we worked well together and decided what needed doing on each loco, then made a plan as to which direction to go in – north or south.

Perhaps I should point out here that Dave Rigby had a business called Dent Design selling postcards, jigsaws, calendars, posters and associated items. He also started to obtain and sell D1048-related merchandise – i.e. car stickers, badges, etc. – in order to raise our profile. Dave Eddleston was in the motor trade buying and selling cars, so we all had busy lives outside the preservation world.

6

Trusting Times

After Dave Rigby purchased D1048 he formed a trust to safeguard the loco's future. This was called the 1048 Locomotive Trust. Later, however, he decided to broaden this idea and form another larger trust to encompass other owners' rolling stock, etc., especially now we had Dave Eddleston with D1041 under our wing. To this end Dave contacted Geoff Drury, a fellow loco owner, to arrange a meeting to discuss the idea. Geoff agreed and the meeting was arranged with him one evening at Birch Services on the M62. Following this meeting we were invited to see his steam locos, 60532 *Blue Peter* and 60019 *Bittern*, which at this time were located at Healey Mills diesel depot. They were in fact en route to Dinting, being temporarily kept there in secure storage. On Sunday 22 October, we travelled over to the depot to see them and have further discussions with Geoff. We arrived to find both locos inside the depot alongside a Class 40. I must say they looked very rough externally at this point paintwork wise, especially *Bittern*. Geoff and two or three others were busy working on them at the time.

The Sunday after our visit to Healey Mills we travelled down to see Warship D832 and Hymeks D7076 and D7096, which were lying in sidings at Egginton Junction on the Derby–Stoke line. We had last visited them in June 1977 and wondered what state they may be in. The answer, as we expected, was poor; all were looking very weathered and forlorn. This visit did, however, turn out to be significant as we shall see later.

In the following weeks the trust was set up and was called the Northwest Locomotive Trust Ltd. I have a document dated 10 November 1978 listing seven subscribers: Francis Barnes, Michael Marsden, Peter Broadhead, Dave Rigby, Dave Eddleston, Geoff Drury and myself. The trust was actually incorporated on 13 June 1979. As you can see, things were now getting a lot more involved. Incidentally, on 9 September that year there had been a meeting in Birmingham of loco owners and representatives to form a new group called the Association of Diesel Owners. Those present were Richard Holdsworth, D1013; Colin Massingham, D821; Paul Koch, D7029; Dave Eddleston, D1041; D. Ashley and J. Boothroyd, D1062. John Vaughan was also present by invitation. Dave Rigby was contacted by the group in November with an invitation to either join or support it. At the time I think he thought he had enough on his plate with setting up the trust, etc., so the request was put on hold until he could allot more time to it. In the end this never happened.

Above: D832 *Onslaught*, D7076 and D7096 are seen languishing in the sidings at Egginton Junction on Sunday 29 October 1978. D832 seems to have suffered more vandalism than the others at this stage.

Below: I took the opportunity to climb into the cab of D832 for a look around on 29 October 1978.

As 1978 drew to a close, on the last day in fact, 31 December, during a phone call between Dave Eddleston and Dave Rigby it was agreed to take Dave Eddleston into the trust as a founder member and trustee and it was agreed in principle to the trust taking over the restoration, maintenance and operation of D1041 *Western Prince*. So, in the first weeks of January 1979 various plans swung into action. The NYMR were contacted and they were delighted to offer us a home for D1041 provided that this did not involve any finance from them. This assurance was given and from 5 January D1041 was placed on the accepted engine list. The loco could move to the railway at any time to suit both parties. Bill Jeffries at Swindon Works was contacted to form an agreement between the works and ourselves to get D1041 into a fit-to-run condition before transfer to the NYMR. This proposal was approved and D1041 was placed inside the weigh house for battery charging and the pre-heaters to be checked over, etc. The loco would be fuelled, watered and the engines would be run up. It would then be checked over and driven in the works yard. When both parties were satisfied, the loco could be moved up north. George Hembury at BR Bristol was contacted for the freight charge from Swindon to Grosmont to be calculated, with a possible move date between the end of February to the middle of March. A programme of work would be drawn up after its arrival at Grosmont, then if all was well a full repaint was to be carried out at the end of the year (possibly into golden ochre livery). A running agreement was also proposed to be drawn up between the trust and the NYMR that any monies raised would be allocated back to D1041 to help with maintenance and the like. Dave Eddleston was very pleased with all this activity towards his engine after essentially being on his own up until now.

7

Feeling the Cold

Alongside the time being spent on trust matters, we were also making plans for the future of *Lady*. The question of a repaint came up a few times and after much discussion we decided on BR green. This livery had been carried by some members of the class in the early years, including D1002, D1003, D1004, D1035, D1036, D1037 and D1038. D1048 had never carried this livery, but we felt it would be a good idea to present one preserved member of the class in green. John Bevan from York was approached to undertake the job. John had previously done work for the National Railway Museum, so we felt fairly confident in employing him. *Lady* would be placed inside the shed at Grosmont in December 1978 for this work to be carried out.

While all this was going on I decided to write to John Vaughan about the idea of him running a railtour using the newly painted D1048 on the NYMR. John had run several railtours with Westerns in their final months, including one with D1048 on 24 February 1977 called the Western Lament. John didn't hang around and, as he was a keen supporter of the class, readily took up the challenge. He then contacted me on 11 December to say that arrangements had been made with BR and the NYMR and the train would run from King's Cross to Malton, then coach transfer to Pickering for D1048 to Grosmont and back. The tour would be called the Western Recall and would run on Sunday 18 March 1979. 'Right,' I thought, 'we'd better get D1048 ready, working and painted by then!'

At this point, I will hold my hands up and say that we were ultimately responsible for what happened next, but hindsight is a wonderful thing, as they say. Looking back, perhaps we should have been more astute at the time. As 1979 dawned, it got really cold and we realised belatedly that after our last visit to Grosmont we hadn't drained *Lady* of coolant. It's easy to look back now and criticise, but at the time all the railway preservation matters had to intertwine with our working and home lives, so it was easy to take your eye off the ball as it were. With it becoming so cold, Dave dispatched a colleague of his who lived in York up to Grosmont to check the loco, but unfortunately it was too late. Despite being in the shed, it had frozen up. I clearly remember Dave ringing me that evening with the bad news. The pressure was really on now to get *Lady* repaired, up and running, and all this on top of a repaint for the forthcoming railtour.

We had a trip up to Grosmont the following weekend to see the damage; there were quite a few engine components with cracks in. We had a good examination and put a plan together. Luckily for us, Westerns were still being broken up at Swindon Works, so after phone calls to Bill Jeffries, visits were arranged to try and recover the parts we needed. We had a total of four visits to Swindon: the first was on 20 January, then on 4, 11 and 18 February, during which time we managed to acquire the necessary spares. It was fortunate at that time I had the use of a works pickup; it helped enormously and was put to good use. Parts we needed included radiator elements, intercoolers, heat exchangers and a turbo, plus various pipe fittings, hoses, etc. We had to strip these parts off locos in the works and off engines and cooler groups lying in the con yard before loading them up. We hired a van to transport the heavier radiator elements and turbo, by which time the poor thing was fully loaded. Unfortunately, on the way home it broke down on the M5, but that's another story! Luckily, Bernard and Dave could devote more time to the job during the week than me, so they would drive up to Grosmont with the spares and unload them. We would then go up at weekends and change over all the damaged parts.

The railtour date seemed to be approaching fast. We worked very hard prior to the tour and progress was not helped by the freezing weather. In fact, the snow and freezing temperatures lasted from January to March and the NYMR had many challenges trying to keep the railway operational. When the thaw came, they had a lot of frost damage to repair at the stations and with infrastructure. In the last week before the railtour Bernard went up to Grosmont in my Escort van with more spares to finish off various jobs and got

Having the use of my works Datsun pickup came in very useful when recovering Western spares from Swindon Works, as in this view taken on 20 January 1979.

D1048 is seen in January 1979 in the rather cramped Grosmont shed having just been repainted by John Bevan. Some of the plastic sheeting can be seen hanging up, which he used to form a tent over the loco while he carried out his work.

snowed in whilst up there, even having to walk through deep snow to get to his B&B each day. Meanwhile, John Bevan had done a wonderful job on the repaint of *Lady* despite the cold weather and cramped conditions in the shed.

The weekend of 17/18 March arrived, and we were really hoping luck was on our side. After our arrival on the Saturday morning all checks were made, and the pre-heaters were switched on. The loco was warmed up and then, after the usual starting procedures, the button was pressed and it fired up. Both engines ran well – phew! After a period of running and various checks we were happy with the results of our labour.

On Sunday 18 March we woke up to yet more snow. After a quick breakfast we went to the shed and prepared *Lady* for the special day. After leaving the shed and a shunt or two we set off for Pickering and encountered some quite deep snowdrifts en route. Had drones been invented at this time it would have been possible to obtain some superb footage of this trip. After our arrival we attached the loco to the stock and waited for our passengers to arrive. In the back of my mind, I was hoping that no issues would arise on the tour's trip up from London. There were no mobile phones of course in those days to check. There was about an hour's delay, however, due to the Malton–Pickering road being impassable, so the train had to go to Scarborough, with passengers duly conveyed by coach to Pickering. Incidentally, the train loco was 40119. Our passengers duly arrived from Scarborough and boarded the train. John Vaughan came up to the front of the loco, attached the headboard, then walked to the side and poured champagne over the front of *Lady* to mark the celebration of this special occasion. We thought it was a lovely gesture.

With everyone on board, we departed for Goathland with a photo stop at Levisham. The train had to terminate at Goathland due to re-sleepering work between there and Grosmont. However, this did not spoil the day in any way. The trip went well and *Lady* performed faultlessly. With Kim Malyon's assistance we even had the steam heat boiler working. During the stop at Goathland we had some lads from the Western Locomotive Association up in the engine room to see what we'd been up to. They were amazed at what we'd achieved in such a short time and we were very grateful for their comments.

Back at Pickering, we uncoupled from the stock and headed back to Grosmont while some very happy people made their way back to London. On arrival back at Grosmont we put *Lady* to bed and drained down the coolant. We weren't taking any more chances!

During our three-hour drive home, we reflected on the weekend's events and were very satisfied with how things turned out. We always referred to this tour as the 'snow trip'. As a point of interest, a picture of the tour made it onto the front cover of the January 1980 edition of *Railway Magazine*. It was the icing on the cake to see *Lady* in the snow on the cover of this popular magazine.

I feel I must mention that during this period Kim Malyon (shed master) and Norman Ash (traction inspector) were very helpful towards us, although steam was inevitably their top priority.

Lady is seen at Newbridge Crossing on 18 March 1979 having encountered some deep snowdrifts en route from Grosmont. Bernard can be seen on the left watching proceedings as it passes.

Above: As we wait for the 'Western Recall' participants to arrive on 18 March 1979, I take a minute to have my photo taken with *Lady*.

Below: Many happy people take the opportunity to take photos of the loco before heading back to Pickering, 18 March 1979.

Our next trip out was a HST special to London on 31 March (organised, I think, by the NYMR). After our arrival in London we nipped over to Paddington and caught a train out to Swindon for a quick look around the works again. D1041 was noted outside 'A' shop with its engine removed and cabs sheeted over, while the gutted shell of D1012 was under the con yard gantry awaiting final disposal. A number of Maybach engines were also noted lying around the area.

On 31 March 1979, D1041 stands at Swindon Works minus an engine and with its cabs sheeted over.

8

And Then There Were Three

Our next trip out was to the Severn Valley Railway for their Western Day on 1 April with D1013 and D1062 both running, which was most enjoyable. Then, over the Easter weekend of 13–15 April we were back up at the NYMR with D1048, where it ran a few trips – some the whole length of the line, some from Grosmont to Levisham and back – and again ran without any trouble. *Lady* also worked on 5 May, but we were unable to attend on that day as we had a trip down to see D832 and the Hymeks at Egginton Junction again. Dave Eddleston also came along in his red Triumph GT6.

British Rail were to hold an open day at Swindon Works on 19 May, so we went down on Sunday the 6th to help Dave Eddleston work on D1041 to get it in a more respectable condition ready for display. Rubbing down and painting were the main tasks of the day. Whilst we were there the Diesel Traction Group had D7029 running and were moving it on and off the turntable at the front of the works. D818 and D821 were also present.

The following Sunday, the 13th, we had another trip down to see D832 at Egginton Junction. This time we cheekily decided to take some yellow paint with us and paint the nose ends to hopefully improve the appearance of the loco, which was now standing alone in the sidings with one wagon looking in an increasingly vulnerable state.

On Saturday 19 May, we were once again at Swindon Works with D1041. This time for the open day D1041 was placed on show between the weigh house and the main works building, where many photos have been taken of diesel hydraulics over the years. We had a sales stand alongside the loco and one of its name and number plates on show, along with a set from D1048 (which I owned at the time). People were allowed into the cab for a small donation and there seemed to be plenty of interest as to what we were hoping to achieve. *Prince* looked quite respectable after its repaint, including red buffer beams despite the bogies being untouched and the job being hastily done due to time constraints.

Interestingly, four days after the open day on 23 May, *Lady* worked the annual weed-killing train from Grosmont to Pickering and back. Sadly, we were unable to witness this, but you can't win them all, as they say.

Having previously purchased a loco from BR, Dave Rigby was on their tender list for further locos and stock as they became available for sale. One evening in April 1979, he rang me to say he'd received a tender form and said, 'You'll never guess what it's for.'

Above: *Western Lady* is seen at Grosmont during Easter weekend on 13–15 April 1979.

Below: Dave Eddleston poses with his Triumph GT6 holding my D1048 number plate whilst on another visit to see D832 and the Hymeks at Egginton Junction on 5 May 1979.

We had another visit to Swindon on 6 May to work on D1041's bodywork to make it look more respectable for the forthcoming open day.

I pondered for a minute and said, 'Go on, tell me.' He told me it was for D832 *Onslaught*. Dave wasn't going to bid for it himself but wondered if we wanted to tender for it through the trust. I said I would think about it and contact him soon. I spoke to Bernard who, like me, could not bear to see the loco go to the scrap man, which would be a real possibility. He agreed with me that we should have a go at trying to buy it, but realistically we hadn't got the money, so we decided to ask Malc if he wanted to join us in our quest. He thankfully agreed, so we now had to try and raise some funds between the three of us.

A few things came into play during the days that followed, including how much should we bid and how were we going to raise enough capital to buy it? After some discussion we decided to try and find out a rough scrap price and bid above it, but this would be a complete gamble on our part as the scrap man would just bid on 78 tons of scrap metal while we had to be a lot more cautious. We also didn't know if any other group or person would be bidding on the loco as well. In the event of us being successful in our bid, we decided our only course of action would be to get a loan to pay for it. From memory, I think the three of us could only manage to raise about £1,100, which would be well short of the amount needed to buy the loco. As the time grew nearer to return the tender form, we decided to bid a figure of £3,800, bearing in mind there would be VAT to pay on top of that amount as well. We filled in the form, sent it off and waited. In all honesty, we were not very hopeful of a successful outcome.

Above: Bernard, Malc and I had a further trip down to Egginton to see D832. Knowing its plight, we decided to take along some yellow paint to try and spruce it up a little. We didn't know at this stage whether our efforts would be in vain, but thankfully they weren't. This photo taken by Dave on Sunday 13 May 1979 shows the three of us with the loco – Bernard has the paintbrush in his hand.

Below: A photo taken later in the day on 13 May 1979, after we painted both yellow ends. The loco was looking very isolated on its own in the sidings.

Above: Looking more respectable, D1041 stands ready to greet the crowds for the open day on Saturday 19 May 1979.

Below: *Western Prince* creates a lot of interest at the open day on 19 May 1979 and is flanked by our sales stand and displays.

BRITISH RAILWAYS BOARD
SALES ACCEPTANCE

25 May 1979

SALES REFERENCE 52/230/521T/006/01

1048 Locomotive Trust
Mr D Rigby
45 Castlecroft Ave
Blackrod
Nr Bolton
Lancs

IMPORTANT: PLEASE READ ALL INSTRUCTIONS. Any variance from the terms of this sales contract must be agreed with the Director of Supply before materials are released.

The sales reference must be quoted on all communications.

Your offer to purchase the following has been accepted, subject to the Board's General Conditions of Contract BRB......18...and/or as stated on our tender form/s.

VAT is not included in the price quoted below; this will be added to the invoice.

VEHICLE LYING AT: Eggington Junction

TERMS OF PAYMENT: Cash before commencement of operations. Only after receipt and clearance of payment will release authority be given.

PRIOR ARRANGEMENTS FOR REMOVAL/CONSIGNMENT must be made with: Director of Research, BRB Railway Technical Centre, Derby. Tel: 0332-42442 Ext: 2320

INVOICES: Please send payment, in accordance with the attached invoice/s, to the Treasurer, British Railways Board at the address shown on the invoice, enclosing the remittance advice — no covering letter is necessary.

Item No.	Description	Approx. Quantity	Price (excl. VAT) Unit......Each....
3	REDUNDANT LOCOMOTIVE Loco No 832 "Onslaught". Class 42 "Warship" Class Diesel hydraulic locomotive. This locomotive has been stripped of various panels and suffered some damage due to vandalism. Price as and where lying, purchaser to undertake dismantling (where necessary) loading and removal at his own expense and leave the site in a condition acceptable to the British Railways Board's representative. ASBESTOS - Tests have been carried out on this vehicle and these would indicate that blue asbestos is not present. However this does not constitute a complete guarantee that blue asbestos or any other form of asbestos does not exist in this vehicle and it is the responsibility of the purchaser to confirm this during work on the vehicle, taking appropriate action if asbestos is found.	1	£ 3800.00

METHOD OF DISPOSAL: Clause ..B. below applies to this sale.   YOUR REFERENCE

This material is sold as and where lying. You are responsible for loading WITHOUT ASSISTANCE FROM BR STAFF, and removal by road at your expense. Sorting on site is not permissible. Your vehicle/s to be weighed both before and after loading on the nearest BR/Public weighbridge in the presence of a BR representative, who must retain a copy of the weigh ticket. Material must be cleared promptly on receipt of advice from the Board.

This material is sold as and where lying. You are responsible for any dismantling necessary, loading WITHOUT ASSISTANCE FROM BR STAFF, removal at your own expense, and leaving the site to the satisfaction of the Board's representative.

Delivery will be made carriage paid by the Board, by rail to nearest available station or siding served by British Railways at:—

Material as loaded into rail wagons, where lying i.e. you to pay carriage charges in addition.

*DELETE AS NECESSARY

This acceptance is issued by:
Director of Supply,
Railway Technical Centre,
London Road,
DERBY DE2 8UP
Tel: Derby 42442 ext....3450.. Telex: 37367
VAT Reg. No. 232 1646 92

SIGNED........
R D READ   for DIRECTOR OF SUPPLY.

BR 8290/45

The piece of paper that changed everything for us three lads – all in our twenties at the time.

On 25 May, a sales acceptance letter was sent to Dave stating that our bid had been successful and that *Onslaught* was ours! After the news sank in, we had to sort out payment of course. We now realised we needed the extra finance, so we decided to approach Yates Burgess Finance Ltd in Manchester – our reason being that they had handled a similar situation with Dave with his purchase of D1048. They agreed to our request and the paperwork was drawn up. The total price we paid for D832 was £4,104. This was made up of a deposit of £1,104, which left a balance of £3,000 to be paid back at £110.85 per month for thirty-six months. This would ultimately cost £3,990.60. Add to it our deposit and a grand total of £5,094 would have to be paid to own D832. This was a massive amount of money to three ordinary working lads like us. However, we managed to pay BR for *Onslaught* on 1 June 1979, which was a Friday, and we travelled down to Egginton Junction to see it and take some photos on this historic day. I think the magnitude of what we had achieved and were about to achieve finally hit us. No going back now, lads!

A Potted History of D832
Built: 1961 Swindon
Into traffic: 8 February 1961

Allocations
Plymouth Laira   February 1961 – July 1961
Newton Abbot   July 1961 – June 1965
Plymouth Laira   June 1965 – September 1965
Newton Abbot   September 1965 – August 1967
Plymouth Laira   August 1967 – October 1971
Newton Abbot   October 1971 – January 1972
Plymouth Laira   January 1972 – November 1972

Withdrawn: 16 December 1972
Total mileage: 1,131,000

Note: D832 arrived at Derby under its own power on 10 January 1973 to be used by the Research Centre but during its time there had very little use.

As a matter of interest, my own first sighting of D832 was at Newton Abbot depot on 1 October 1966 whilst on a spotting trip. Little did I know then how things would unfold years later.

On Sunday 3 June, we went back to the NYMR as D1048 was needed for a roster. This roster was rather strange as the loco would work the first train of the day out of Grosmont as far as Goathland, then uncouple for a steam loco to take over for the rest of the trip to Pickering. We would then retire to the siding until doing the reverse working back to Grosmont later in the day. The weather on this particular day was pleasant, so we used the layover time to give the loco a clean and do some maintenance tasks.

D1048 stands in the sidings at Goathland during its layover period between services on 3 June 1979.

9

Here, There and Everywhere

Having been successful in purchasing D832 we were very concerned about its vulnerability at Egginton Junction, knowing what the vandals had done and could still do to it, so we decided we had to act quickly to get it to a safer location. With the help of Dave Eddleston and others, it was agreed and arranged that we could take it to Derby Etches Park, which was only a few miles from where we were. This movement was arranged for Thursday 7 June – just six days after we paid for it.

On arrival at Egginton that morning we were approached by the signalman, who said he had some items off the loco that had been confiscated from the various characters who had been inside it and removed them. These items included handbrake wheels and various gauges and fittings. We were very grateful for this gesture. We made our way over to the sidings and found D832 with a brake van attached. 25320 soon arrived from Derby to tow us away. 47228 then arrived with a rake of mineral wagons, which it recessed into a siding adjacent to us in order to let a passenger train pass. It then went away towards Derby. We had a chat with the guard and boarded the brake van and shortly afterwards we moved off slowly towards Derby. During the trip we passed 47080 *Titan* and 46052 both on passenger trains and 56018 on a merry-go-round train. On arrival at Derby, we were shunted into the DMU servicing sidings at Etches Park, after which we left the depot and made our way home. D832 would later be moved to the fore shed at the back of the depot.

Three days later, on 10 June, we were back at Derby to start work on D832's bodywork. We decided our priorities were to make it look respectable and get it watertight. Also, some glass in the cabs and engine room had been smashed and needed replacing. On our arrival we found D832 at the back of the depot sharing siding space with a stranger from the Southern Region in the shape of 74010, which was there temporarily whilst en route to Doncaster for scrapping. We made a good start on this first working day but were mindful of the task ahead. Dave Eddleston was very helpful to us, especially living in Derby. He was able to source replacement glass and various bits and pieces. The keen-eyed people among you will have noticed the engine room windows in D832 are a one-piece glass instead of the original two-piece ones. This is because we simply couldn't get two-piece ones with the time and resources available then. Mind you, the replacement ones have been in the

Above: A busy period at Egginton with 47228, 25320 and D832 all sharing siding space prior to our departure to Derby on 7 June 1979.

Below: 25320 and D832 and a brake van ready to leave for Derby on 7 June 1979.

Above: A view from the brake van as we approach Derby on 7 June 1979.

Below: D832 after arrival at Derby Etches Park on 7 June 1979.

loco now for over forty-five years, so can't be too bad! On this and all subsequent working days at Derby, once we had finished working we would retire to Dave's house for tea. There was always a good spread waiting for us, put on by his good friend Brian, before we headed home.

At this time, it must be remembered that five of us now had not two but three diesel hydraulics to look after in three different parts of the country – D1041 in Swindon, D832 in Derby and D1048 at the NYMR – and we had our home and working lives in between. I don't know how we managed, but somehow we did.

On Thursday 14 June, we were back at Swindon Works doing jobs on D1041 and collecting some spares. Three days later, on the 17th, we were at Derby again working on D832. This was followed by visits on 24 June, 8 July, 14 and 15 July and 29 July. The next week, on 4 August, we were up at Grosmont on D1048; this time it wasn't an operating day, but we had the loco running and moved it up and down the yard. General maintenance was also undertaken. At the end of the day we buffered up to Class 31 D5500, which was there at the time on loan from the NRM. We shut the loco down and had our usual three-hour drive home. The next day, Sunday 5 August, we were down at Derby again working on D832, followed by a further visit on 19 August. Around this time we learned that the works were to hold an open day on 1 September and we were invited to display our loco. This, however, put us under a lot more pressure to get the loco painted, etc., in time. It would only be able to appear in undercoat, but at least it would be show-worthy, we thought.

With some glass in the cab and headcode boxes, D832 begins to look much better. Photographed on 8 July 1979.

Above: Activity surrounds D1048 at Grosmont shed. Dave Eddleston is also in view in this image from 4 August 1979. This was a general maintenance day for us.

Below: D1048 moves towards D5500 at Grosmont on 4 August 1979 prior to being shut down for the day.

Throughout this period, I had been in correspondence with Michael Harris at *Railway World*, who was interested in our progress with D832. On 3 July, he sent a letter to me regarding this, followed by another dated 26 July, to say he would feature the purchase of D832 in the 'Preservation Scene' section of the October issue. In this piece I had requested that if anyone had any warship cab fittings, etc., that they may be willing to donate to us to please get in touch. It was also stated in this article that we hoped to have D832 running within a year. I now think that was wildly optimistic! We were also featured in the July and November 1979 issues of the *Railway Magazine*. In the latter article it was stated that we had purchased a Class 45 diesel hydraulic loco, but I'm sure that was a typing error!

Following these articles we received various letters from well-wishers, some offering cab parts, spares, and such. Some offered practical help and wanted to join our group. The problem was we really didn't run a group or society: we didn't have the time and it would mean a lot more organisation. The five of us would just decide what to do and where to go and just get on with the jobs in hand. However, we did have occasional help from family and friends.

One person who contacted us was Mike Woodhouse, a fitter at Laira at the time. He had previously worked at Old Oak Common, so knew his way round diesel hydraulics well. He was a great help to us, offering aid, advice and information during the following months.

One letter I received was from a gentleman offering us two warship nameplates: *Majestic* ex-D830 and *Conquest* ex-D603 at £450 and £550 respectively. This was a good offer, but times were tight moneywise so sadly we had to decline. As a point of interest, during my time with D832 we were never offered either of its original nameplates. They must be out there somewhere, I expect.

The morning of Saturday 1 September arrived and we were once again at Derby. This time though we could enjoy the fruits of our labour as D832 was proudly on display at the works open day. Although it appeared in a light green undercoat, it looked very respectable. There was an information board (which I still have) placed next to the loco by the works staff for added interest. We received many favourable comments about the loco and we were very pleased with the day's proceedings.

We were even more pleased to learn that after the open day D832 was to be kept in the works yard, not taken back to Etches Park where we had been paying a weekly siding rent. This move also gave us breathing space as things had been rather pressured in the weeks leading up to the open day.

As I mentioned earlier, Dave Rigby and Dave Eddleston were on the BR tender list since they had previously bought locos. On 24 September, we had a trip down to Bristol Bath Road depot to see the only surviving Co-Bo D5705 (or TDB968006 as it was known then), which had been put up for tender. We were not going to bid for it but wanted to take the opportunity to have a look around it. It had suffered some fire damage at this time and looked rather neglected. Fortunately, it was later saved for preservation and is now to be found at the East Lancashire Railway undergoing a lengthy restoration.

After a break for my holidays at the end of September, it was back to work with my daily agricultural machinery job and at the same time dealing with loco preservation matters. I dealt with all the correspondence regarding D832 and our group, answering letters from companies and people. Anything to raise our profile was my goal. In October 1979, I was in contact with General Mills UK Toy Group in Coalville, who had the mainline railway division. They had produced a nice 00-gauge model of D824 *Highflyer* and I enquired if

Above: It's Saturday 1 September 1979 and *Onslaught* is proudly on display at Derby Works open day. We were really pleased to see it looking so well after all our hard work over the last few weeks.

Below: 45062 and D832 on display at the open day on 1 September 1979.

they would be willing to do one of *Onslaught*. Their response was very favourable, and they said they would hopefully produce one at a later date. One was eventually produced by Bachmann when they took over the mainline warship range, so a good result in the end.

Our next trip was up to D1048 on 14 October, where it was on one of the rosters for the day. All went well, as usual.

Towards the end of October, we were approached by Derby Works, who enquired if we would be interested in their apprentices painting *Onslaught* in topcoat as a training exercise. The only stipulation was that we would have to provide the paint. As you can imagine, we were delighted to take up their offer! This work would be carried out on an 'as and when' basis and would have to be done in between their own pre-planned work. We understood this and the deal was done. It also suited us well as we were in no hurry to move the loco away at this time, having not identified a home for it yet. We contacted the well-known Williamsons company, who had supplied paint for BR in the past. They were very obliging, and plans were set in motion.

We visited Derby Works on 4 November to check over D832, which was stabled in the works yard amongst various Class 45 peaks. Interestingly, 44008 and 44009 were also present, the latter sadly awaiting scrapping. D832 stood out against the other locos in its light green livery. On 18 November, the two Daves, Bernard and I were once again up on the NYMR. This time we were at Pickering, where D1048 had been stabled. We did a full day's work on the loco, including some bodywork repairs. We returned home tired but happy with what we had achieved.

D832 is stabled in the works yard amongst various Class 25 and 45 locos on 4 November 1979.

A moment in time captured as Dave, Dave and Bernard get stuck into some bodywork repairs on *Lady*. The damage to the bodyside is very prominent in this view from 18 November 1979.

Dave Rigby owned a Volvo Estate car during this period, which came in very handy for taking tools, spares, etc., up to the NYMR. On one occasion we hired a steam cleaner, which was loaded into his car for the trip to Pickering. Having unloaded it, we set to work on various parts of the loco. We were disappointed though, as anyone who has worked inside a Western will tell you they were covered in a layer of black super grime, which the steam cleaner failed to dislodge. We later had to resort to other methods to tackle the job on further visits to the loco.

In November, I received an insurance quote for D832, which I had requested from British Engine Insurance Ltd. As a matter of interest to readers, it read: 'Machinery to be insured Diesel Hydraulic Locomotive *Onslaught* sum insured £170,000 annual premium £595.' This was to cover extraneous damage, fire and theft with seven exclusions. Additional cover for the steam boiler, steam piping and seven air receivers would cost another £246 annually. Needless to say, at the time we decided – rightly or wrongly – to postpone any decisions in this regard to a later date.

In early December, work commenced on D832's bodywork and it was placed inside the paint shop, where it remained until after the Christmas period as the work progressed. Again, we were very happy that (a) the work was being done for us and to a professional standard and (b) that the loco was under cover for the first time in years, which we thought was a very good situation to find ourselves in. It was at this time we had the advantage of having an electrical power supply available and this enabled us to eventually power up the loco lighting circuits. We found all the lamp fittings intact and every one worked. It was only a minor thing, but it would have been the first part of the loco to be powered up since BR service. The warm glow from the engine room was matched by our moods.

On 16 December, we travelled to Pickering again to work on D1048. It would be the last trip of the year. Various maintenance tasks were carried out during the day to ensure it was in a good state. We drained it down again, so it would be safe until we could return in the new year. What happened next turned out to be very significant and proved to be a turning point as further events unfolded.

One evening in December my phone rang and the caller said, 'Hello, is that Mr Crowther?' to which I replied, 'Yes.' He then introduced himself as Phil Southern from the East Lancashire Railway and politely asked if we had secured a home for *Onslaught* yet. I replied, 'No, not at the moment.' He said that was the news he was wanting to hear and that he would hopefully offer us a home at the ELR. He invited us to a meeting at the ELR, to be arranged in the new year, to formulate plans for both parties and we would take it from there. Little did we both realise that this phone call would eventually result in what is now the Bury Hydraulic Group alongside other diesel groups at the ELR, which is now a major player in the heritage railway world in the UK.

Bernard and I stand proudly in front of D832 in the paint shop on December 1979.

Dave and I are pictured with D832 in the paint shop in December 1979.

10

Onwards and Upwards

The year 1980 would prove to be a very busy one for me and our small group in many ways. As it dawned, we were off on New Year's Day to York to see restaurant car E1937, which had come up for tender. Our idea was that it would be a useful vehicle at some point in the future to go into a dining train – we were full of ideas at this point! Malc met us there to look around the vehicle, then took us around York MPD where Deltics 55016 and 55021 and various other locos were under repair. We found this very interesting.

Restaurant car E1937 is seen at York on New Year's Day in 1980. We had travelled over to inspect it with an idea to purchase it for possible inclusion in a dining train; sadly this never happened.

Five days later, on 6 January, we were down at Swindon with D1041. It was in the weigh house on this occasion with an 08 shunter. Various jobs had been done on it by the works and hopefully looked to soon be running again. We sorted some spares this day too so that we could return in the week to collect them.

Four days later, on 10 January, Bernard, Dave Rigby and I were once again at Swindon. We were in a hire van this time to collect various Western spares that we had put aside in the con yard. Also in the yard was BG parcels van M31274, which Dave had purchased for use as a spares storage vehicle. This would hopefully move with D1041 when the time came. As a matter of interest, on this day D1041 was sharing space in the weigh house with steam loco 5051 *Earl Bathurst*, which was in there for weighing.

Following the phone call from Phil Southern in December, Dave and I went to a meeting at Bury at the ELR on Saturday 12 January. The meeting was very fruitful, and I think it's fair to say at this time the facilities, like most other preserved railways, were fairly basic; essentially there was just the old goods shed in Castlecroft Yard, which had very tight radius lines to access it. It seemed to us only small rolling stock, such as 0-4-0 tank locos and four-wheel wagons, would be ok but not much else. We enquired as to whether they might accommodate our loco (or possibly locos). 'No problem' was the answer, as they would be willing to build us a shed! 'Wow,' we thought, this was ideal as it clearly showed real commitment on their part. They proposed building a shed by the tunnel next to the Castlecroft Yard with straight access from the running line. Subsequently, this is exactly

Dave and Bernard are pictured on 10 January 1980 at Swindon Works with a hire van which we had loaded with various western spares.

Above: Bernard and I, both covered in grime, stand with the van on 10 January 1980.

Below: Parcels van M31274, which Dave had purchased, stands in the yard at Swindon Works on 10 January 1980.

D1041 is seen in the weigh house on 10 January 1980 with 5051 *Earl Bathurst*. This building is now a restaurant.

what happened. The shed is still fulfilling this role to this day, housing hydraulic locos. We came away very pleased as it was apparent that both parties wanted each other. Phil said he would keep me informed of the progress, which he did. The next day, the 13th, we had a Northwest Locomotive Trust meeting at Dave's house in Blackrod, then the following day Dave went up to the NYMR to check on his loco.

Six days later, on the 20th, we were back down working on D832 at Derby, which was still in the paint shop and now wearing a light grey undercoat. Malc did some electrical work while Bernard and I attended to some jobs in the engine room. Dave Eddleston was busy painting in the A-end cab. To our dismay, we discovered some slight vandalism in the B-end cab, which wasn't good. Later, Malc got the train back home while we drove home – after we'd been to Dave's for tea, of course. One week later, on 27 January, we were once again back at Derby with just me, Bernard and Dave Eddleston in attendance. D832 was now in a green undercoat. Again, Bernard and I were in the engine room while Dave did more painting in the cab. He told us that Swindon had contacted him about repainting D1041, but he hadn't decided to go ahead with it at this point. Another visit to Derby was made the following week and more small jobs were completed. On 4 February, Phil Southern contacted me to let me know their latest proposals regarding the shed. They were now going for a three-road shed which we both agreed would be perfect.

On 10 February, we were back down in Derby again. D832 was now outside, parked amongst the Class 25s and 45s. There were six of us present on this day, working inside the loco rubbing down, painting, etc. Malc was working on the electrical side as usual. This visit was followed up by another a week later with just three of us in attendance. We finished a little earlier this day and went to see Hymeks D7076 and D7096 at Old Dalby in Leicestershire on our way home. Both locos were looking in a sorry state at this time and we pondered as to what their future may be. Eventually, after the two locos were no longer required by the research centre, they were disposed of. Happily, D7076 was bought for preservation and later joined D832 at the ELR. After yielding many spare parts for D7076, however, D7096 was scrapped in Sheffield in 1986. The fact that D832 and D7076 were used by the research centre eventually led to their preservation, which we must be very grateful for. Had the locos not been kept for research purposes, they most certainly would have gone the way of their sisters and been scrapped in the early 1970s.

Our next working party was on Sunday 24 February, when five of us went up to D1048 at Pickering. On this occasion it was parked in the head shunt between the station and the road. Some work on this day included horns and covers replaced, various relays freed up and/or removed for repair, pre-heater stacks refitted, brakes adjusted, engines barred over, the loco cleaned externally, inner skirts cleaned, plus attention to the front air tank straps. As anyone involved in loco preservation will tell you, work of this kind is not always easy when the loco is parked outside open to the elements with no facilities to call upon. You just have to crack on and get the job done.

Seen on 27 January 1980, D832 still resides in the paint shop at Derby but now sports a light green undercoat, making it look a lot more respectable.

Above: Seen on 10 February 1980, D832 has been placed outside in the works yard amongst various diesel electrics.

Below: Dave is busy masking up and measuring the new nameplates on 17 February 1980. 45023 *The Royal Pioneer Corps* can be seen behind.

Above: Bernard can be spotted perched on top of D1048 attending to a pre-heater during one of our working days. The loco was stabled in the head shunt at Pickering on 24 February 1980 – not really the ideal location for such maintenance work.

Below: D1048 stands in the head shunt at Pickering on 24 February 1980.

There were two bits of news on 29 February. Firstly, Mike Woodhouse rang to say that he had secured a Maybach lifting bracket for us at more or less scrap price that would have to be collected from Plymouth Laira depot. Secondly, Phil Southern rang to say things were progressing well with the shed project at Bury. On Sunday 2 March, Dave and I went down to Laira to collect the lifting bracket, which was kindly arranged by Mike who came to the depot with us to assist loading. The following day we took the bracket up to Bury where Phil Southern greeted us once again. As this would be our future home, Dave was hoping to get D1048 moved there soon as well and was in negotiation with the NYMR regarding this matter. The following Sunday, 9 March, we went up to Pickering again to continue working on D1048. On this occasion there were six of us in attendance: me, Bernard, Malc, Dave Rigby, Dave Eddleston and Paul Marshall. We filled it with coolant and, after some trouble with the A-end pre-heater was sorted, it fired up no problem. We had it running for quite a while as various other tasks were carried out during our visit. At the end of the day *Lady* was shut down and drained before we left for home.

In February I had been in contact with Horwich Works as we had been informed they were to be holding an open day in August. I thought that they may be interested in having D832 and possibly D1041 as exhibits; this would give them some added attractions and provide us a temporary base until the shed at Bury was ready. I thought it was a case of 'if you don't ask, you don't get'. On 12 March, I received a letter from the works management stating they would be delighted to have us. Of course, we were very pleased with this news.

D1048 receives further attention to its bodyside damage at Pickering on 9 March 1980.

Meanwhile, D1041 had been having work done on it during the past few weeks, so on the 13th Dave went down to Swindon and witnessed his loco running on both engines. Whilst speaking to him that evening I could tell he was extremely happy. Three days later four of us went down to Swindon to meet him. D1041 was still inside the weigh house and we did various jobs on it here during our visit. Interestingly, we had a walk around the con yard while there and found very few Western spares lying around. We could see five transmissions, six bogies and a few engines. I suppose it wasn't too surprising at this stage that there was so little left. A few days later I contacted Swindon regarding those remaining items, enquiring if any of them would be for sale, but they told me they were all sold for scrap. During previous visits we had enquired about the possibility of buying one or more transmissions and one or more bogies, but were told that we wouldn't ever need them when the locos were running on preserved lines at line speeds of around 25 mph. We took their advice and didn't pursue the matter, but in hindsight I think we should have tried to save some, as they would have been invaluable in today's preservation world, even just for use as spare parts. As we now know, D1010, D1015 and D1023 have had transmission troubles since being preserved.

D1041 in the weigh house at Swindon on 17 March 1980. Bernard and Malc can be seen kneeling on the floor by the doors at the back. I'm not sure what they were doing, but something is keeping them occupied.

11

Testing Times

In the six weeks leading up to the week beginning 24 March I had been receiving snippets of information regarding Dave Rigby's financial matters. I became increasingly concerned, so discussed the situation with Bernard, Malc and Dave. My then wife Linda worked for him in his souvenir business and there had been missing wage payments. I also found out various loco spares had not been paid for, and I even heard suggestions that D1048 was in fact not owned by Dave! Sadly, during this period I felt that Dave had been less than truthful with us for some reason. Matters came to a head on 25 March when I received news that his business had gone into liquidation. This was quite a shock, and I wondered what the coming days and weeks would bring. I had a meeting with him on the 28th where he told me that he had plans to extricate himself from his financial difficulties. Meanwhile, my own finances were in a bad place at this time. Despite working longer hours one week, I was left with a mere £10 until my next payday. This was compounded by my wife now being on the dole due to Dave's business going bust. Bad news wasn't only confined to us, as Bernard had also now become unemployed. It never rains but it pours!

Despite all the doom and gloom, things were progressing well with our loco and we scraped the petrol money together for another visit to Derby on the 30th. D832 was now back in the paint shop, masked up ready for its topcoat of green. We subsequently found out that unfortunately Williamsons had supplied the wrong shade of green. Luckily, however, someone in the works had located the right shade of paint, so the job could now proceed. We would have to return the wrong paint to Williamsons in the near future. I also contacted Dave Newton of Newton Replicas who agreed to supply us with new name and works plates for D832.

Meanwhile, down at Swindon things were progressing well with D1041. It was almost finished and Dave decided to explore movement costs in order to join forces with us and come to Bury, which we were delighted about. Dave Rigby rang me on 1 April to say he'd received a movement notice for the BG spares van at Swindon and hopefully it could come up with D1041. I thought this a little curious due to his present position. Two days later, Dave Eddleston informed me that D1041 had been examined and was ready to move, and also that D832 was now in a shiny green topcoat. The next day Bernard, Malc and I went down to Derby to see our loco, which looked fabulous despite having some scaffolding

In this view from 30 March 1980, D832 is seen inside the paint shop with Peaks on either side.

platforms around it. We were told that they hoped to complete the job in around a week's time. This duly happened. On 9 April, Dave rang me excitedly and said that D832 was now finished and looked magnificent. This was great news; we made plans to go down and see it the following Sunday – the 13th. On arrival we found it sitting outside the paint shop in the sunshine. It really did look superb. We were very pleased with the finished job, as were the apprentices. We took a few photographs of this historic occasion before driving home later in the day, very happy lads indeed.

Things were really heating up for me at this time. Luckily, my employer was very understanding. As stated previously, we didn't have the luxury of mobile phones then and I had phone calls day after day regarding our locos, many during working hours, which of course were taking away calls from J&S Lewis's busy phone lines. I was also in contact with BR at Swindon, Derby and Horwich Works concerning the movement of D832 and D1041. This was all on top of the matters with Dave Rigby and D1048.

Dave Rigby had some business to attend to in Twyford, so I took the opportunity to go down with him on Monday 21 April. While there, I was able to collect some warship items that a man had contacted us about. After this we went to Swindon Works again and noted that as the necessary work had been completed on D1041, it was now coupled to the BG van ready for movement. We also found Warship D818, due to be repainted, located in the weigh house.

Above: D832 is seen on 4 April 1980 in its shiny topcoat of paint, which unfortunately was found to be the wrong shade. This was later rectified.

Below: D832 stands proudly on display after being completed by the works' apprentices on 13 April 1980. A similar scene could have been experienced at Swindon in the 1960s.

D1041 and the BG van are coupled together ready for onward movement from Swindon on Monday 21 April 1980.

Malc, Bernard and I were very uneasy with our position with the finance company Yates Burgess, as we didn't want to be caught up with anything relating to D1048. Ours was obviously a separate agreement with the company, but we decided it might be in our best interests to try and pay off the loan for D832. On 23 April, I contacted the company to ask for a settlement figure and the next day received a letter from them stating that it was £2,537, to which my immediate reaction to this was 'how the hell are we going to find the money?' This couldn't have happened at a worse time really, but we needed to resolve things somehow. A little bit of good news came this week, however, as I managed to find Bernard a job at a sweeper hire firm in Warrington. It was a place I had previously worked at, and Bernard was, needless to say, very pleased. The firm operated lorry sweepers around the area.

On Friday the 25th, after yet more phone calls, it was agreed Malc would stump up the lion's share of the loan and I would find the rest. I did have one side of D1048's plates in my possession, which I sold to a good friend of mine, Stuart (he still has them to this day). I also had a steam loco number plate and some other bits which I sold to a dealer. In fact, I sold anything I could to raise the money.

On Sunday the 27th we went down to Derby to meet Dave Eddleston who had kindly collected *Onslaught*'s new nameplates for us. We trial fitted them and they really did

YATES BURGESS FINANCE LTD.

Directors:
J. Hollingsworth, M.A., F.C.I.B.
N. Brown
P.H. Edgerton, Secretary

74 KING STREET
MANCHESTER
M2 7AX
Tel: 061-832 7531

Also at:
The Rotunda Birmingham B2 4AG
Tel: 021 643 9387

6 Latimer Street Romsey Hants SO5 8DG
Tel: (0794) 513826

30 Winter Hey Lane Horwich Bolton BL6 7AA
Tel: (0204) 693211

FIRST CLASS.
S. Crowther Esq.,
8 Mason Close,
Ashton-in-Makerfield,
Cheshire.

Our Ref: SMT
Your Ref:
Date: 23rd April, 1980

Dear Sir,

Re: Agreement No. M/830A - Warship 832 'Onslaught'.

With reference to our telephone conversation I would advise you that the settlement figure for the above account is £ 2,537.00 if received by 6th May 1980. I have contacted the bank with regard to the April payment and am advised that they are awaiting a further credit before this can be forwarded to ourselves.

With regard to the question of the insurance, we have no alternative but to take out insurance on this engine, the cost to be met by yourself, should settlement or alternatively proof of adequate cover not be received by 6th May 1980.

Please advise us of the present location of the engine.

Yours faithfully,
YATES BURGESS FINANCE LIMITED

S.M. TIMS (MRS).

Vat No. 147 1018 92   Consumer Credit Licence No. 042560   Reg. Office: 74 King Street Manchester M2 7AX Reg. No. 634585 England.

This image shows the letter from Yates Burgess regarding the settlement figure and probable insurance costs.

look good. They were finished with a black background instead of the usual red. D832 was now once again stabled with various other locos in the works sidings. During the next day at work, I was contacted by Neil Brown from Yates Burgess to say that *Western Lady* had been repossessed. This was bad news that we had not wanted to hear. With the cheque for D832 now ready, mainly thanks to Malc, Bernard and I took it to Neil Brown on 29 April – at the time it felt like we'd paid for the loco twice. As a matter of interest, I had received a letter from Yates Burgess informing us that if the account had not been settled by 6 May, they would take out insurance on the loco and the cost would have had to be met by ourselves. They also wanted to know the location of D832. Thankfully, we had just avoided this situation by a few days, proving to us that we had done the right thing by paying the loan off. I'm sure the situation with D1048 had some bearing on our situation, as previously nothing had been said or implied regarding insurance and the location of our loco. However, it was reassuring to receive a letter from them on 7 May stating that the loan had been fully paid up and the 'goods' were now our property.

While all this had been going on I was regularly in touch with Terry Foley at Horwich Works who was very helpful towards us, mainly keeping him informed of progress. I had also been in contact with Tony Quirk of the Rocket 150 Committee to see if there was any chance that we could get D832 in the forthcoming cavalcade at Rainhill. I received a letter back from them on 3 May declining our offer. I had thought there was only a very slim chance of it happening, but it was worth a try. At least D1062 *Western Courier* appeared there, which was a good representative of the diesel hydraulic classes.

D832's new nameplates have now been fitted. We had them finished in black rather than with the usual red background and thought they suited the loco well. However, we later changed them back to red. Seen on 27 April 1980.

Resplendent with its gleaming paintwork, D832 stands out amongst the other locos in the works yard on 27 April 1980.

On 4 May, Neil Brown went up to see D1048 at Pickering. Then, three days later, Malc went with some BR colleagues to examine it for movement to wherever Yates Burgess may request it to go. The company had placed little white stickers along each side of the loco that stated, 'These goods are the property of Yates Burgess Finance Ltd'.

On Monday 12 May, I received paperwork and receipt from Yates Burgess which concluded our financial matters with them. On a personal level, I noted that again I only had £3 to last me until payday on the following Friday. For various reasons, my finances were really tight at this time.

12

Pastures New

It's funny really, but Yates Burgess were of a different mindset since our completion of financial matters with D832 and contacted me regarding D1048, asking for help and advice, which I was happy to give. They had also been in contact with the Western Locomotive Association regarding the loco. I had an interesting call from Neil on 15 May who stated that the Dart Valley Railway had offered £12,000 for D1048, which they had declined, and also that the NYMR had wanted the diesel fuel taken out of it. A further charge would also be made to move the loco from Pickering to Grosmont, ready for onward movement away from the railway. I think they felt somewhat aggrieved at the way the loco was leaving, which, to be fair, you couldn't blame them.

Knowing of our situation with D832 and D1041 going to Horwich, Neil Brown enquired if he could take D1048 there whilst a new buyer could be found. As they were based in Manchester, I think they wanted it in the north-west where the sale could be handled more easily. He told me that the company had previously repossessed cars, boats and even an aircraft, but never a 108-ton railway locomotive! The managers at Horwich agreed that the loco could be taken there, so BR was contacted and on 21 May D1048 left the NYMR, arriving at Horwich two days later. Incidentally, the same day D1048 left, D1062 was taken to Wigan Springs Branch depot for fuel. It was in the area to take part in the Rocket 150 celebrations. Two Westerns on the move in the north-west within a couple of days – not an everyday occurrence!

Things were still moving apace with our own loco and my phone kept ringing. Phil Southern contacted me on 22 May to say a shed building had been located for us and that it would be delivered to Bury on the 25th. Dave Eddleston was also busy contacting BR at Paddington and Crewe in an attempt to get D1041 moved from Swindon to Derby, then on to Horwich. There was a problem trying to get a path over the Hope Valley route apparently. He had, however, been successful in obtaining a spare Western transmission from Swindon, which was good news. He rang me on 2 June to say that he now had a moving date for both locos: 9 and 10 June. I then informed Terry Foley at Horwich of this news. We made arrangements between ourselves regarding what we would do while the move took place and arranged time off work and accommodation in Derby for the Monday night. Malc came over on the Sunday to stay with me overnight. The next morning we

D1048 is seen at Horwich after its arrival from the NYMR on 23 May 1980. The little white stickers along its bodyside had been placed there by Yates Burgess stating in no uncertain terms who the loco belonged to at this time.

picked up Bernard and drove down to Abbotswood Junction, near Worcester, to wait for D1041 and the BG van to be towed up from Swindon with Dave on board. We waited for about four hours, but no Western appeared. As there were no mobile phones in those days, wondering what had happened, we went to see the signalman at Norton who told us the move had been cancelled. You can imagine our reaction. We decided to drive up to Derby as originally planned and take things from there. Dave eventually arrived to join us after having travelled down to Swindon and back by train. He explained to us that the driver had failed the Class 25 loco rostered for the move, which meant the original plan had to be postponed by twenty-four hours. He was not amused as he had arranged for the local press to be around when his loco arrived, so it also upset their plans. Having complained, he did in fact get his train fare refunded. Bernard, Malc and I of course had to inform our employers that we would be a day late getting back to work. Situations like this affect many other things, as many of you will know. There is always a knock-on effect.

The next day Dave travelled down to Swindon again, keeping his fingers crossed. Malc took his car back to York while Bernard and I tinkered on D832 for the day until he returned by rail. D1041 and the BG arrived at Derby at around 6 p.m. It then took us over three and a half hours to get the shunters to move D832 from the works yard to Etches Park and buffered up to D1041. Although the two locos were only a stone's throw apart, a certain amount of bureaucracy intervened which prevented an easy and less time-consuming move.

D832 and D1041 are finally marshalled together at Etches Park on the evening of Tuesday 10 June 1980, ready for onward movement to Horwich the following day. D832 is now sporting red nameplates.

The next morning, 11 June, we woke up to a rainy day. We went over to Etches Park and Malc, Bernard and I climbed aboard D832, with Dave in D1041, ready for our trip to Horwich. We left at 8.30 a.m. behind 31315. Whilst en route, we had stops at Ambergate, Dore, Edale and finally Chinley, where 31315 was detached and 40067 coupled on for the remainder of the journey. At Chinley, my good friend Stuart Cameron and his BR driver friend, Ivan, were waiting for us with a reporter from the *Buxton Advertiser* who had been asked to record the event. Following this, Stuart and Ivan jumped aboard and accompanied us to Horwich. Malc left us at Manchester Victoria so he could make his way home to Yorkshire. We arrived at Horwich at 4 p.m. It had been a successful trip despite the wet weather. Dave, Stuart and Ivan hitched a lift back to Manchester in 40067. Bernard and I went back home and returned later to secure the locos. Neil Brown was also at Horwich this day with, I believe, Roland Hatton and others working on D1048. They had removed the batteries for charging and were working in the cabs. I must say, *Lady* was looking rather rough externally.

The following day whilst at work repairing a clutch on a four-wheel-drive tractor, Neil Brown rang me implying I'd said detrimental things regarding Roland and others working on D1048, etc. I don't know where that came from. Dave Eddleston also rang and said he

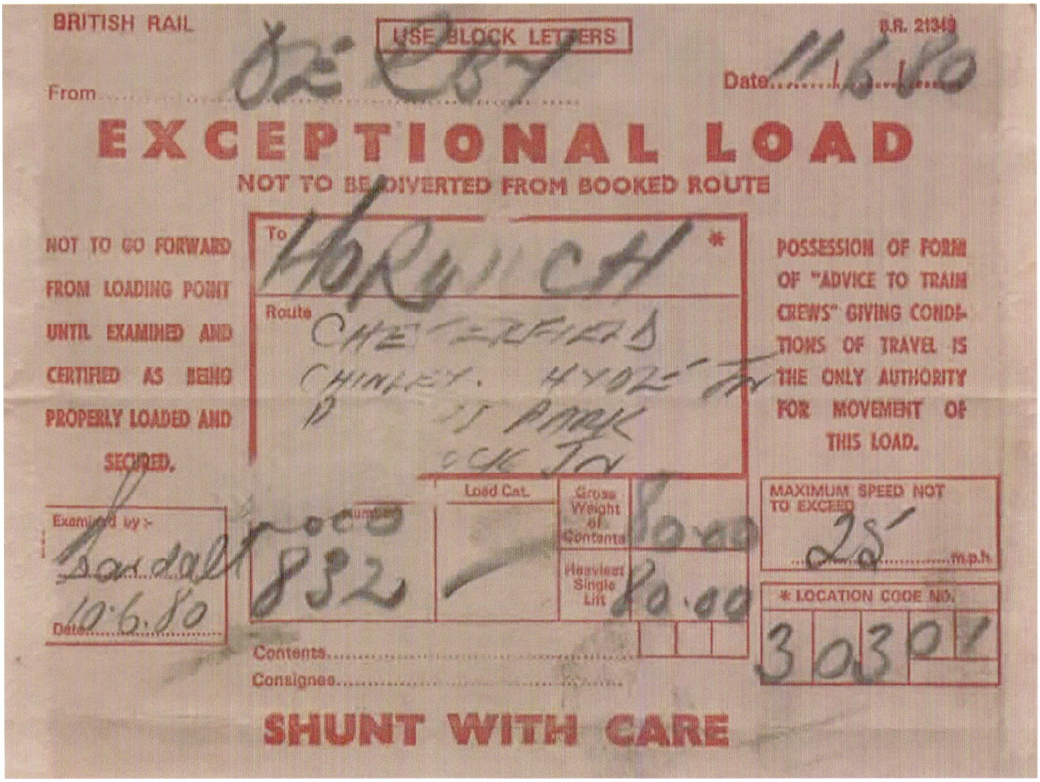

BRITISH RAIL	USE BLOCK LETTERS		B.R. 21349
From D832		Date 11.6.80	

EXCEPTIONAL LOAD
NOT TO BE DIVERTED FROM BOOKED ROUTE

NOT TO GO FORWARD FROM LOADING POINT UNTIL EXAMINED AND CERTIFIED AS BEING PROPERLY LOADED AND SECURED.	To HORWICH * Route CHESTERFIELD CHINLEY. 4Y02 TO D ST PARK OCK JN	POSSESSION OF FORM OF "ADVICE TO TRAIN CREWS" GIVING CONDITIONS OF TRAVEL IS THE ONLY AUTHORITY FOR MOVEMENT OF THIS LOAD.
Examined by :- Sardalt Date 10.6.80	Number Loco 832	Load Cat.	Gross Weight of Contents 80·00	Heaviest Single Lift 80·00	MAXIMUM SPEED NOT TO EXCEED 25 m.p.h. * LOCATION CODE NO. 3030
	Contents............... Consignee...............		

SHUNT WITH CARE

Above: This was the movement notice affixed to D832.

Below: Hauled by 31315, we pause at Ambergate for an hour in the drizzle while waiting for a clear path across the Hope Valley on 11 June 1980.

Above: Dave looks out from the cab of his loco during another stop at Dore on 11 June 1980.

Below: After a loco change at Chinley, 40067 is attached for the next part of our journey to Horwich on 11 June 1980.

had spoken to Neil and Roland. I can't honestly remember the details now, but I felt pretty hacked off with it all and thought that if this is preservation, you can stick it! I certainly didn't want any added grief whilst at work, that's for sure. That night I had five different people ring me, one of whom was Dave Rigby. He spoke for almost an hour about matters concerning D1048 and said he was going to contact Neil again about it. I thought, 'Blimey, we've only been at Horwich for twenty-four hours, we don't need aggro like this.' I spoke to Roland the next day to iron out any misunderstandings and the matter was resolved.

Two days later, on the 15th, Dave came up from Derby and he, Paul, Bernard and I went up to Horwich. Dave and Paul worked on D1041's cab while Bernard and I worked on D832's pre-heaters and headcode doors. On the evening of 18 June, Bernard and I went up to Horwich to meet Phil Southern and friends for a look around the locos and have a chat about forthcoming events at Bury. We also obtained official entry passes for the works at this time. The following night Bernard and I were at the works again cleaning under the cab floors of D832 and painting D1041's horn surrounds. I must say, it was now a lot easier for us to work on the locos with them not being far from home. We could, and did, go up after tea on quite a few occasions.

13

Money and Politics

On 20 June, Dave Eddleston rang me to say that he'd had a letter from BR Bristol wanting payment for movement of the BG van and D832 to Horwich *before* their movement. We thought they were a little bit late for that, seeing as the move had already taken place nine days previously! Seven days later, he contacted BR at the centralised accounts office in Nottingham to sort out the movement fee on our behalf; however, he essentially got nowhere, and we would have to wait for the invoice to arrive. Also on this day, Dave Rigby contacted me and said he would be getting *Lady* back. This was followed by another call from him on 15 July, when he told me that he had now got *Lady* back and that the lads and I had let him down and he would no longer be bringing the loco to Bury. I was disappointed he felt that way about us after all the work we'd done on the loco for him, but I think at this time he had been under a lot of pressure which perhaps affected his mood. With regards to the loco itself, I thought: 'Well, we will just have to wait and see what happens.' On a more positive note, the next day Phil Southern rang me to say the foundations were now dug out, ready for the erection of the shed. In the week beginning the 14th we had been up to Horwich twice and made ready both turbos for lifting off in D832.

Throughout this period some WLA members had been working on D1048, and on 24 July it was placed in the paint shop for further work and a repaint to be carried out. Also, on this day Roland told me that he had been informed that a man was coming next week to see it running. This man turned out to be Mr Jim Kaye.

Meanwhile, we had been busy on D832 and D1041. On D832, we disconnected the turbochargers ready for lifting off as they were both seized. Roland told us that he could get a crane if we required it, which we thought was a nice gesture and that's how things should be – i.e. groups working together for a common goal. We worked on D1041's bogies, trying our best to remove rust, scale, brake dust, etc., in order to repaint them and the rest of the loco in readiness for the forthcoming open day. Malc took the batteries out to give them a service and charge up. On 27 July, D1041's batteries were refitted, the engine filled with coolant, the yellow end repainted and various other jobs done.

At around this time one of our local newspapers, the *Newton and Warrington Guardian*, contacted me and wanted to do an article about us and D832 prior to the open day at Horwich, where they considered *Onslaught* would be a star attraction. So, on Saturday

2 August, a reporter and photographer came to Horwich and interviewed me and Bernard (unfortunately Malc was unable to attend). The following week the article appeared in the newspaper with the headline 'It's a Jolly Green Giant' along with a couple of photos of us with the engine. We were pleased with what had been written – fame at last!

The following weekend we continued our work on D1041, painting the bogies, roof and bodywork. There were six of us in attendance and by the end of the day, although not professional in any way, we were very pleased with the result. *Prince* would indeed look good for the forthcoming open day. In the week leading up to it we went up each evening after work to sort various jobs including, hopefully, getting some fuel into D1041 as we hoped to get it running and moving up and down on a short section of track. The day before the open day I had the day off (yes, another one!) and, along with Bernard, we prepared the locos for their big day. We did manage to get some fuel into D1041, which was good. Also, D1048 had been rapidly repainted; this was very last minute, as I believe there had been some uncertainty with regard to Dave Rigby saying he was getting the loco back.

On Saturday 16 August, Horwich open day was upon us. Mike Woodhouse had travelled up from Devon to be with us for the event and Malc had come over from North Yorkshire. We had a very busy day, and our locos were proudly on display. We had D1041 running on both engines and moving up and down a short distance, which pleased the crowds. The event was a big success, with many thousands of people in attendance.

D1048 is outside the paint shop at Horwich the day before the open day, ready to be shunted in for a quick repaint. Seen on 15 August 1980.

Above: D1041 and D832 look lovely in the evening sun on 15 August 1980, ready for the crowds the following day.

Below: D832 stands proudly on display at the Horwich Works open day on 16 August 1980.

Left: Malc, Mike, Bernard and I pose in front of D832 after the visitors had left at the end of the day.

Below: Echoes of the 1960s as D1048, D1041 and D832 stand quietly at Horwich on Sunday 17 August 1980.

Later, Dave Rigby became involved with the Liverpool Road Exposition in Manchester, which began on 1 August. He rang me on the 26th saying he would like to get D832, D1041 and D1048 to attend. He also wanted to obtain a pre-heater for D1048.

The next few weeks were a bit strange really. Dave Rigby was adamant he was having *Western Lady* back and mentioned this to me a few times during phone calls. Then we heard that Mr Jim Kaye was buying it. I think the WLA had stopped working on it as no one seemed to know what was going on, so we arranged a meeting with Mr Kaye on 1 September.

While we were working at Horwich on 31 August, Dave Rigby turned up and went inside *Lady* and disconnected one of its pre-heaters as it had a split water jacket. It later turned out that both pre-heaters had split water jackets, so both would need removing for repairs. The next day we met Mr Kaye as arranged and had a good chat with him. He was interested in *Lady* and, as expected, wanted to know all the facts and figures before attempting to buy it. In the end he never did, but unfortunately I have no details as to why. A few days later, Dave Eddleston rang me to say that Dave had contacted him and wanted us to work on *Lady* again and get it working. Also, he had been informed of outstanding accounts from Swindon Works: £3,000 for engines and £1,700 for a bogie. Until these amounts had been paid neither D1041 nor D1048 could move from Horwich. We didn't recollect Dave Rigby buying these items, but he must have said he wanted them, although we certainly weren't aware of any details of this arrangement. On 24 September, Dave Rigby came to see me about us getting involved with *Lady* again, but I wasn't prepared to commit any of us to this at that time.

Two days later, a large invoice arrived through my letterbox from BR for the movement of D832 from Derby to Horwich. The total invoice amount was £1,654.14 and they wanted remittance by return of post. They also stated that this should have been paid before the loco was moved but said that this had been inadvertently overlooked. I took a deep breath and wondered again how on earth we would pay for it. Fortunately, Dave Eddleston came to our rescue. He approached the Divisional Manager in the accounts office at Nottingham, with whom he'd had previous dealings, and after some negotiation on our behalf he got the amount owed reduced to £402.50 inclusive of VAT. As you can imagine this was great news, and we sent the money off immediately. We had helped Dave a lot with his loco and I think this was a way of thanking us, which was much appreciated, I can tell you.

On 28 September, three of us were at Horwich with Dave, who had driven up from Derby to find Dave Rigby there with some lads from the Deltic Preservation Group working on *Lady*. They tried to get it running, but the batteries were flat. He told us he was taking the loco to the Liverpool Road exhibition site in Manchester where he could get it operational again. I believe this is when Neil McCannon and Terry Waterhouse became involved. On 2 November, when Bernard and I visited Horwich he was once again there trying to start *Lady* with the help of Neil and some lads from the Liverpool Road Museum, but once again the batteries failed. Prior to this, Neil had organised both pre-heaters to be repaired and reinstalled in the loco. We drained D1041 down for the winter on this visit and also covered the exhaust and pre-heater stacks with plastic. This was followed by another visit a week later when Bernard, Malc, Dave Eddleston and I found Dave Rigby and the Liverpool Road lads once again attempting to start *Lady*. We did give them a hand on this occasion and managed to get it running on one engine after a lot of effort.

With her future yet to be decided, D1048 resides at a temporary home at Horwich on 28 September 1980.

Following this, we went over to Bury to find the shed structure was now up. Phil Southern greeted us as usual and told us they now had the keys to Bolton Street station and that the coal merchant at Rawtenstall had been in touch with the railway about the possibility of moving coal over the line. Things were really progressing well. Having sorted things out financially with BR at Swindon, Dave Eddleston wanted his transmission moved out of the works, so I asked our local haulier Eric Massey if he would collect it for us, which he did on 27 November after arrangement with Bill Jeffries. The next day, Eric pulled up in his articulated lorry in the yard at work and asked, 'Where do you want this gearbox?' I managed to borrow a large forklift from the shipping company next door and we lifted it off and placed it inside the tractor workshop. The following Sunday, Bernard and I went in to work and completely cleaned up the transmission ready for a repaint. Jim, the boss, didn't like the look of a rusty lump of iron sitting in the workshop with customers coming in and out. The following Saturday we painted it in undercoat, then the next day, 7 December, we applied a topcoat of grey and I must say that it looked very presentable. When we had finished, we drove up to Horwich to find Dave Rigby with Neil and the lads there and they had *Lady* running on both engines and the steam heat boiler working as well. He told us that his loco would be moving away at the weekend to the Liverpool Road site. To be honest, I took this with a pinch of salt. Then, on 11 December, Dave Eddleston received a letter from Swindon releasing D1041 for movement, which he was very pleased about. On 21 December, Malc came over to see the transmission in our workshop, after which we went up to Horwich and barred the engines over in D1041 and had a general check over our locos. Needless to say, D1048 was still there, which didn't surprise us at all.

 **British Rail**

British Rail (London Midland Region)　　Revenue Accountant,
　　Phone : 0602 48531　　　　　　　　Centralised Accounts Office,
　　　　　　Ext. 2396　　　　　　　　　Furlong House,
　　　　　　　　　　　　　　　　　　　Queens Drive;
　　　　　　　　　　　　　　　　　　　Nottingham. NG2 1AL

Mr.S.Crowther,
8,Mason Close,
Ashton in Makerfield;
Lancs.

y/r
o/r　　A12/4748　　　　　　　Date　11th.November 1980

Dear Sir,
　　Account No.916075 Week 36 1980.
Consignment Note No. 0026 22 0367
Privately Owned Locomotive From
Derby to Horwich also Examination
of same.Charge £1654.14 V.A.T.
inclusive.

　　Thank you for your payment of £402.50
and accompanying letter dated 7th.November 1980.
　　I now enclose Credit Note No.F12/510 for
£1251.64 V.A.T.inclusive for your records.The
account has now been cleared in full.

　　　　　　　　　　　　　Yours faithfully,

　　　　　　　　　　　　　for Revenue Accountant.

BR 1/12

This is the letter I received from BR relating to our move from Derby to Horwich, which, thanks to the intervention of Dave Eddleston, was much reduced.

14

Turning the Corner

In 1981, our first visit to Horwich was on 4 January. Dave Eddleston also came up from Derby to see his loco. Dave Rigby and his team were there and once again had D1048 running, which was good to see. The very next day, Monday 5 January, Dave Eddleston was contacted by Swindon who told him that money was still outstanding for the spares that Dave Rigby had taken. I thought, 'Here we go again!' On the same day we found out that *Lady* was still up for sale and Yates Burgess wanted £41,000 for it! This didn't quite tally up with Dave's version of him saying he was getting it back.

With things now progressing well at Bury, we decided to contact BR at Preston to ask for a quote for the movement of the locos from Horwich. Subsequently, on 7 January they sent an inspector to examine the locos, which had been moved into the paint shop. Malc came over from Yorkshire as he he'd had experience of this procedure previously and so could assist with any technicalities which may occur. Both locos passed the inspection, but it was stipulated that they could not travel to Bury via the third rail, so would have to go via Castleton and Heywood. Phil Southern and I were in touch with each other regularly regarding any developments at either end, so he was pleased with this news.

On 24 January, I received a letter from BR quoting us £800 plus VAT for the movement of the locos to Bury, which we were happy with, so arrangements were put in motion for the move. It would take place on 11 February, although Phil had wanted it to take place the previous week, but this had proved impractical.

Meanwhile, on 31 January, we loaded the Western transmission onto our works lorry at Culcheth and delivered it to Bury. The weekend before the move we were at Horwich preparing the locos for their journey. This included charging up the batteries on D1041 and repairing an air pipe. We also gave D832 a good wash, even though it was raining steadily. We wanted them to arrive in Bury in style.

On Wednesday 11 February, we were at Horwich Works with the locos for a 9.10 a.m. departure. We eventually left at 10.45 a.m. The weather was typical: cold, foggy and sleety with a few odd bright spells. The train loco was booked to be a Class 25, but in fact 40115 turned up, which we didn't mind at all. Unfortunately, Malc didn't make the move with us because his car broke down in Leeds. Strangely enough, as we passed Manchester Victoria the sun came out briefly; anyone there would have got a nice shot of us passing through.

Above: It's 31 January 1981 and the Western transmission has been safely loaded onto the lorry at Culcheth for transport to Bury courtesy of Jim and Steve Lewis. Jim can be seen on the left while Steve is on the forklift.

Below: Having arrived at Bury, the transmission is slowly lowered onto the waiting wagon on 31 January 1981.

Above: Bernard is busy giving D832 a wipe down in the rain on 8 February 1981 at Horwich prior to its move to Bury.

Below: D832 and D1048 stand side by side for a final time at Horwich on 10 February 1981. They wouldn't meet again until September 2023 at the Severn Valley Diesel Gala some forty-two years later.

The trip passed without incident and we arrived at Bury around 1 p.m. The television crews were there to greet us and Dave Eddleston did an interview. The interesting thing was that after our arrival the track had to be slewed across to gain access to our new shed. Both locos had to be winched in with block and tackle, but there were plenty of people on hand to help. During this operation D832 became buffer locked with one of the brake vans, but at the end of the day both locos were safely under cover at their new home. Job done.

The following Saturday, the 14th, there was a DMU special that ran up to Rawtenstall, so we took the opportunity to have D1041 running up and down from the shed to the halt and back with Malc driving. This would be the start of many happy years on the East Lancs Railway.

In the weeks that followed we would usually go to Bury on a Sunday and attend to various jobs on the locos as required. We also started to attend courses on railway procedures, etc. We were now entering another phase of our preservation journey. I noted we had a very busy day on 29 March. Work included taking the roof sections off D832 and removing the air filters, from D1041. At this time Phil was quite excited about the prospect of Bulleid Pacifics 34010 and 34027, Black 5 45407 and a Class 25 coming to the railway.

On 31 March, Mike Woodhouse contacted me to say that the Plym Valley Railway were going to try and raise the money to buy D1048. This was interesting news as I knew that there were at least two other parties interested in buying the loco. We would have to wait and see.

40115 is seen prior to departure from Horwich with D832 and D1041 on the very misty morning of 11 February 1981.

Above: A view from the cab of D832 as we approach what was Manchester Exchange which, as can be witnessed in this image from 11 February 1981, is sadly being demolished.

Below: Some discussion takes place on 11 February 1981 as D832 has become buffer locked with the brake van. The problem was soon resolved.

With the two hydraulics safely in their new shed, 40115 moves away on 11 February 1981.

Each weekend in April, myself, Bernard, Malc and his friend Andy, Paul Marshall and sometimes Dave Eddleston worked on D1041 and D832. Also around this time, Neil McCannon came along and joined our team. He had been working on D1048 at Horwich and had obviously enjoyed it! To provide further insight into the tasks we undertook, on 5 April Bernard and Paul were stripping D1041's A-end cab for refurbishment while Neil and I were in the engine room taking the gangways up and degreasing, etc. The following week it was a repeat procedure: Bernard and Paul were in the cab while Neil and I were in the engine room again. On 10 May, we had a full team working on D1041: myself, Bernard, Malc, Dave, Paul, Neil and Andy. This was great, with us all working together to get the jobs done.

15

A Change of Direction

By the end of May 1981 my home circumstances were changing quite rapidly and so my priorities changed. This resulted in my decision to step back from front-line preservation. I would, and still did, go up to Bury, but attending week in week out was now at an end. I know both Bernard and Malc were disappointed, but looking back now I can see that it had been basically full on for me over the past few years. In a sense our goal had been achieved. We'd bought *Onslaught* for preservation, moved it around the country and found it a secure home for the future, which we could be very proud of.

As I previously mentioned, the Plym Valley Railway were actively seeking funds to buy D1048. Ken Chinnock was the chairman of the diesel group and after he'd been in contact with me I offered to be their liaison officer at Horwich Works should they be successful in their bid. As I lived fairly locally it was a lot easier for me to be of assistance, practical or otherwise. Despite all previous events I still had a lot of affection for *Western Lady* and still do to this day, so I was happy to help. This group had also enquired with BR about the possibility of purchasing Warship D818, *Glory*, which had been lying at Swindon Works for several years. BR's response was that if it was going to be offered for sale it would be put up for tender in the usual way. In the end, as most people know, it was stripped for spares and sadly scrapped in 1985.

On 25 January 1982, Ken received a letter from Yates Burgess stating that their bid had been successful. As the year progressed, Ken organised some working parties to Horwich to work on *Lady* and I did help them occasionally. Hugh Searle and Graham Gant from the WLA had also carried out some work on *Lady*, including barring over the engines, carrying out electrical checks and repairs. Battery, fuel supply and pre-heater issues were also attended to. Ken mentioned that it would be better for D1048 to be under cover somewhere until it could be moved south to Devon and asked me where the nearest sites were in the north-west. I said to him that the only possible places I could think of would be Bury (although at this time there were no possible undercover facilities available), Southport or Carnforth. In the end, after some negotiations, Southport was chosen as an interim home. Even though this had been agreed, *Lady* didn't move there until 27 July 1983, by which time it had been at Horwich for over three years. I did witness this movement, having nipped out of work, and saw it pass through Gathurst, near Wigan, behind 47223. Following this I visited Southport on three occasions to see D1048 but not to work on it.

Above: After various jobs had been carried out, D1048 stands in the afternoon sun at Horwich in March 1982. If I remember correctly, the item under the sheet was a battery charger.

Below: Ken Chinnock can be seen on the roof of D1048 in March 1982 sheeting it down before heading back to Devon.

Above: D1048 shivers in the snow at Horwich on 22 December 1982.

Below: D1048 is captured passing Gathurst, near Wigan, behind 47223 whilst en route from Horwich to Southport on 27 July 1983.

Curiously, during its time at Southport in 1984 the previous owner, Dave Rigby, was still making plans to try and get *Lady* back. He contacted me several times between May and July to say he was raising the money and wanted a meeting with Ken Chinnock. This, however, did not happen. He then told me on 16 July that a friend of his was going to try and buy *Lady*. This was followed by another call on 26 July to tell me that his friend was now going to buy a Class 40. This then finally put an end to his plans and the idea was dropped. He certainly wasn't going down without a fight!

D1048 finally moved south on 11 July 1988, having been at Southport for five years. It did have a stop at Plymouth to attend the Laira Open Day on 17 July. It then migrated further south to the Bodmin & Wenford Railway, arriving on 7 August. It stayed there for five years, during which time a large amount of work was carried out on it. However, in 1993 it was sold on again, this time to pop mogul Pete Waterman, who had it transported by road to Crewe on 23 November. His plan was to overhaul it and hopefully bring it back to mainline running standards, but this proved too expensive, so after a period of time it was sold again to Mark Koch and Pete Simpson. They then located it at the Midland Railway Centre, Butterley, for over twenty-five years until October 2023 when they donated it to the Western Locomotive Association at Kidderminster on the Severn Valley Railway. D1048 has certainly had a very chequered history since being bought from BR in 1978.

An unusual place to find a Western. D1048 creates some interest at its temporary home at Steamport, Southport, on 31 July 1983.

My own circumstances changed again in 1983. In December that year I moved down south to Newton Abbot in Devon, which ironically had been the old stamping ground of the hydraulics. Having moved south, I considered my situation regarding D832 and concluded it would be in the loco's best interest if I sold my share of it to Bernard and Malc, which I duly did. I thought it unfair and impractical to keep my share in it as I now lived so far away and wouldn't be able to do any regular work on it. I knew the loco would now be in safe hands.

There was, however, a hydraulic not very far from where I now lived. This was D1023 *Western Fusilier*. Although belonging to the National Railway Museum, it was now located on the Dart Valley Railway at Buckfastleigh. The loco had been on the Dartmouth line for a while and had visited the Laira open day in April 1982. Even though the loco was looking smart in maroon livery, a repair was needed to one of its engines, which had a cracked liner. Mike Woodhouse was approached to do the work and with the help of a hired crane, the engine was lifted out for repair on 19 November 1983. The repairs were carried out over a period of months in 1984 as time and work commitments permitted. After moving to Devon, I assisted Mike with this work and on 26 August we had the replacement liner and piston back in the engine. It was December before we had the engine refitted into the loco. This took place on the 7th – again, with a hired crane. During 1985 more work followed on the loco, and on 24 June we had it running on both engines once again. A test run to Staverton and back took place on 3 September with Mike on board. On 5 September, the loco left the railway for another visit to Laira for the open day, which took place on 7 September. It returned to Buckfastleigh two days later along with DVR stock.

I later became involved with the Class 50 Society when they purchased 50049 *Defiance*. Already having known Mike Woodhouse, Chris Holland, Richard Holmes and David Clough, it was an easy decision for me to join the working parties at both Laira and later Williton on the West Somerset Railway. After all, preservation is a common cause or, as I see it, it should be.

16

Conclusion

Do I think we were naive in taking on D832? Most definitely yes, but at the time we were just driven by a desire to preserve it, and in this we succeeded. Despite the ups and downs, I did enjoy my involvement in loco preservation, even though it was intense and did dominate my life during that period. My time spent in preservation was very brief compared to many other people who have been in it for many years. However, I would like to think I played a part in saving three wonderful diesel hydraulic locos for future generations to enjoy. D832 and D1041 are now owned by the Bury Hydraulic Group at the East Lancs Railway and are in very safe hands. D1048 is now with the Western Locomotive Association, based at the Severn Valley Railway.

In many ways buying a loco is the easy bit. Following this, you must have very deep pockets, a lot of time, patience, skill, goodwill and luck. I get tremendous satisfaction seeing D832 out pulling trains. Having ridden in it and behind it, I have seen the pleasure it brings to people watching it. It has also been a popular loco running on numerous preserved lines. It is a far cry from when we purchased a vandalised and sad-looking loco with seized engines all those years ago.

With regard to Dave Eddleston and D1041, he had it moved to Crewe in 1987 for a body overhaul and repaint into maroon with yellow skirts (as some of the Westerns appeared when outshopped new). Prior to its repaint the loco was on display at the Railway Age Open Day, which the late Queen Elizabeth II and Prince Philip attended. During this event Dave was introduced to them and they took an interest in his loco. Without a doubt this was the highlight of his preservation years. Following this, D1041 was restored at great expense to pristine external condition. The work was completed in February 1988 and afterwards the loco was put on display in the works yard on 4 February. Bernard, Mike, Stuart and Dave Rigby and I went to see it, and it looked superb. The next year Dave sold D1041 to Tim Hanson, then bought 24061 and some coaches, which he subsequently sold on again. His preservation days were now at an end. However, he must be fully credited for having saved three mainline diesel locomotives for future generations to enjoy, which is no mean feat.

A few points of interest here regarding Dave and his locos. Prior to meeting us, Dave had been involved in preservation for a while, having been part owner of steam loco 6960

Raveningham Hall then moving on to buy Hymek D7018. In May 1975, he paid £3,575 for D7018 and £275 for Stones boiler 20374, totalling (with VAT) £4,158. The boiler was located at Cardiff Canton.

On 4 July, D7018 was moved from Old Oak Common to Didcot at a cost of £200. It was towed there by D1025 *Western Guardsman* and Dave was thrilled to be allowed to ride in the cab of D1025 for the trip. Later, in 1975 he was again fortunate to be allowed another cab ride, this time in D1016 *Western Gladiator* from Newport to Cardiff and this really did cement his desire to own a Western, which he achieved in 1977 when buying D1041 *Western Prince*, having paid £5,076 (£4,700 plus VAT) for it. This was not his first choice, however, as he had previously bid on D1009 *Western Invader* and D1005 *Western Venturer* but was unsuccessful on each occasion. He was saddened not to have secured D1009 because it had only been withdrawn with minor defects. In fact, the man who outbid him only wanted the engines out of it. This was a sad loss, as many would agree *Invader* was a very popular loco. When he tendered for D1041 he stipulated the bid must include both its name and number plates – the same as Dave Rigby did with D1048. After his bid was accepted he went down to Collectors Corner in London to collect them. Whilst there, he noted one crest from the unique Class 53 loco 1200 *Falcon* was also present.

After eventually selling D1041, Dave still retained its name and number plates, and he also owned one set off D1040 *Western Queen*. He subsequently sold all three sets of plates to a dealer, which he regrets to this day.

What of the five of us now? Sadly, Bernard and Dave Rigby have passed away. Dave Eddleston doesn't enjoy the best of health. He left the preservation scene some years ago. Malc, having retired from BR, is still flying the flag for us at Bury, where he is a well-respected figure. As for me, I'm still involved with agricultural tractors, as I have been for over fifty years, but haven't been active in railway preservation for some time.

Regarding Dave Rigby: yes, he did receive some criticism in the early 1980s. Some of it may have been justified, but my own view is that at the end of the day he did save D1048 from possible scrapping, which has got to be a positive thing.

Many people helped us on our journey, some of whom have sadly passed away, and I will be forever grateful to them for their help and goodwill. They included Bill Jeffries (Swindon Works), Terry Foley (Horwich Works), Mick, Reg and Paul (painters) and staff at Derby Works, Phil Southern, who was so instrumental in getting us to Bury in the first place, Mike Woodhouse, Jim Lewis, John Bevan, John Boyes, Neil McCannon, Roland Hatton, Stuart Cameron, Paul Marshall, Kim Malyon and Norman Ash.

In early 2005 we held a small ceremony with Bernard's family at Bury's Bolton Street station and unveiled a plaque in the cab of D832 in his memory. This ceremony was filmed by my good friend Steve Marshall (Globe Video Films).

A special event was held at Bury on 1 June 2019 as I wished to commemorate the fortieth anniversary of the purchase of *Onslaught*. Malc, Carl and others made appropriate arrangements for a round trip on the ELR. With the help of my wife, Val, I made a special headboard to mark the occasion, which was attached to the front of D832 prior to departure. With friends in attendance, including Bernard's mother, it was both a poignant and enjoyable experience for us all.

Members of the Bury Hydraulic Group, myself, Josy (Bernard's mother), Malc and others pose with *Onslaught* on 1 June 2019 prior to our departure to Rawtenstall to mark the loco's fortieth year in preservation.

Acknowledgements

The preparation of this book would not have been possible without the help and patience of my loving wife, Val. I must thank her for her unwavering encouragement and enthusiasm in believing that I could achieve my wish to share what preservation can entail. She spent countless hours, following through all the necessary stages and endless amendments, preparing the script ready for submission to the publishers. I will be forever thankful for all her efforts.

I must thank Dave Eddleston, Malc Kirkwood, Neil McCannon and Hugh Searle for their assistance in filling in a few blanks. Thanks also to two accomplished authors, Colin Marsden and Bernard Mills, for their help and guidance.

Also, as a novice writer, I'm thankful to the publishers for their willingness to accept my story. I'd particularly like to mention the Senior Editor Alison Flowers, who has been so supportive in guiding me through the entire process, to whom I'm extremely appreciative.